P. Gorecki, P. Pautsch and T. Lefebvre

Lean Management

Table of content

Introduction 5

1. History of Lean Management 9

2. Guidelines for implementing Lean Management 16
   - 2.1 Understanding the lean philosophy 16
   - 2.2 Added Value 19
   - 2.3 Waste, unevenness, overburden 19
   - 2.4 Value added curve 21
   - 2.5 Implementation 23

3. Kaizen – Continuous Improvement (CI) 27
   - 3.1 Hansei – Necessity of self-reflection 29
   - 3.2 Hoshin Kanri – Policy Deployment 31
   - 3.3 Genchi Genbutsu and Gemba 32
   - 3.4 Lean structure/objectives 33
   - 3.5 Individual improvements 35
   - 3.6 Workshops/teamwork 36
   - 3.7 Internal suggestion scheme 38

4. Visual management – learning to see 40
   - 4.1 Value Stream Mapping (VSM) 40
   - 4.2 Key Performance Indicators (KPI) 42
   - 4.3 Zoning and Andon 46
   - 4.4 Jidoka/First Defect Stop 49

    4.5   Goal and current status 50

5. Pull principle 52

    5.1   Milk Run 52

    5.2   Supermarket 53

    5.3   Small Train 54

    5.4   Production cell WIP 55

    5.5   Shop stock 55

    5.6   Kanban 56

    5.7   Heijunka 57

    5.8   Truck Preparation Area (TPA) 58

6. TPM 60

    6.1   Basic principles 60

    6.2   Involvement of employees 62

    6.3   5S method 63

    6.4   Equipment effectiveness and equipment maintenance . 66

7. SMED - Single Minute Exchange of Die 69

    7.1   Basic principles 69

    7.2   Reduction of set-up times 70

8. Error proofing 73

    8.1   Poka Yoke 73

    8.2   Failure Mode and Effects Analysis (FMEA) 75

    8.3   Total Quality Management 78

9. Sustainable and continuous Kaizen 81
    9.1   Plan.. 82
    9.2   Do 82
    9.3   Check... 83
    9.4   Act/Standard.. 84
    9.5   PDCA and Hoshin Kanri 85
    9.6   A3 report/A3 paper.. 86
    9.7   8D report 87

10. Lean Development... 89
    10.1   U-cells and Chaku Chaku cells 89
    10.2   Cardboard workshop and Minimum Technical Solution... 92

11. Six Sigma 95

12. Tools of Lean Management 97
    12.1   Seven statistical tools.. 97
    12.2   M7 – Seven management tools 106
    12.3   5-W question technique 107

13. Personal commitment – conclusion... 109

Literature.. 111

Introduction

Imagine following situation. You are trying to put a puzzle of 5000 pieces together. On the cover you could already recognize the mesmerizing image which, after all the hard work, would result in the end image of a beautiful tropical island. You are thrilled!

Then, you see the endless stack of puzzle pieces and you would rather not start at all. You have a look at the individual parts and you are able to guess which wonderful scenes have to be combined to form the total picture.

The same applies for managers who stand in front of the "mountain" of parts related to lean methods. They too wonder: Where do we start? Is it sufficient to use one or the other method to or a combination of several to become successful?

Think about it, when you start to put the puzzle together, you look at the different stones and all of a sudden you discover similar elements. You put these together and straight away you find another piece which fits. Slowly recognizable partial pictures start to form, like a palm tree for example. Your motivation to continue increases and out of the chaos of puzzle stones an impressive overall picture starts to grow.

In the same way one could start looking at Lean Management. The company management starts the change towards lean with a vision (a landscape of a tropical island). At that moment, perhaps, no employee sees how the vision will become reality. But, as a leader, if you stand behind your vision and you remain focused on your chosen strategy, then, step by step a lean company will emerge and slowly but surely more and more colleagues will see the vision along with you.

Begin where you can achieve the first successes (the first recognizable puzzle parts) to convince your employees that Lean Management works. Where connecting parts are missing (missing puzzle pieces in the overall picture), there will always be setbacks. The lean methods are very often co-dependent and only function in a combination. Do not let you get distracted from your vision by this, but follow it consequently.

Companies like Toyota have shown us that Lean Management works and can have incredible implications for the profitability and functionality of the business and, more importantly, for the customer orientation of the company.

With Lean Management, costs can be reduced and the economic use of the available resources can be sustained in the long term while increasing customer satisfaction. Lean Management is, in fact, just this: the consistent focus on the customer by reducing to those elements that entail a value for the customer. But what does this mean in practice?

Freddy Ballé (2009) says in his book: "It's all about the people", and that is exactly what Lean Management is all about. Lean Management focuses with the appropriate tools on the customer and their needs. It tries to translate the customer's needs into the language of daily operations.

Every day it makes us stand in front of the mirror to ask us in our own personal language whether we are doing the right thing by visually showing the results of our activities. Lean management tools, in the right application, do not allow dressing up results, leaving us unaffected by HR policy aspects, personal priorities or top management influences.

Lean Management tries to approach people by creating systems that compensate for human imperfections. If one starts from the research results of Mike Rother, then, the human being tends to lose itself in a position between a current state (As-Is) and a future, desired, state (To-Be). The fact that something is physically present does not mean that it is fully implemented or functional. This characteristic of Lean Management guides us through the pitfalls of the not immediately visible hurdles by making them apparent and vehemently challenging us to remove them.

Lean Management and its tools are not there to feed us, but to teach us how we can collect and harvest our own food!

The benefit of introducing Lean Management is a consistent orientation of all (really all) processes in the company to the requirements and needs of the customer. Each activity, process step, administrative activity in the company's operations is measured with respect to its contribution to the customer perceived benefits.

Non-value-adding activities or processes within the company are eliminated. Even if today this doesn't seem possible (because, for example, a warehouse is currently considered absolutely indispensable), this activity will still be considered a waste. The elimination is then a future task.

This book endeavours to convey the philosophy, the principles and the dependencies of the methods and tools of Lean Management in a practice-oriented way. Hereby Lean Management and Kaizen are used synonymously since they are based on the same basic concept/basic philosophy.

The book does not want to teach the implementation of the presented tools and methods. For this, sufficient professional literature is available. The goal is rather to open the reader's eyes for a new perspective and to offer him the opportunity to recognize the incredible potential that Lean Management offers.

For more extended information about Lean Management, the methods and implementation in companies we refer to "Praxisbuch Lean Management – Der Weg zur operative Excellence" from Pawel Gorecki and Peter Pautsch. In 2014 the second German edition has been released by Hanser Verlag (ISBN 978-3-446-44221-4).

1. History of Lean Management

To this day, Lean Management has created some controversy. Since the 1990s Lean Management has been abused by consultants as a cost-cutting program; it has been used as a title in many company programs and projects, in some of these without any correlation whatsoever, from Toyota not used at all (notion) and oft wrongly put into competition with Kaizen. Do Toyota and Lean Management have something in common? Do they belong to a common family of methods or did they arise parallel? Is it the individual, a group or a philosophy that make companies which implement Lean Management so successful? If we have a look at Toyota, we see an example of the rise of an automobile manufacturer which has reached the top of its industry. This was not achieved by acquisitions from other companies or brands, but through the use of the company's own performance potential. Today, Toyota is regarded as the flagship company for a way of working and its corporate philosophy is unrivalled. Lean Management is once again the synonym for the implementation of a philosophy and way of working by this well-respected Asian manufacturer.

But does this way of working and philosophy come from the drawing board of one genius engineer? Was this exclusively developed by Toyota? Was it solely one person who shaped it? Why does this philosophy have such a broad approval status in Lean companies? To understand this and Lean Management, one must know its history. Its origin and the fathers of its origin. This is why we devoted the next part to its history, to show that Lean Management and the Lean tools were coined by many people and that, by their success, they have generated a dynamic on their own.

Referring to the beginnings of Lean Management, we start our journey with Henry Ford, the Toyoda family, which has also founded the Toyota Motor Corporation, and we will have a closer look at the Asian culture. Furthermore, William Edwards Deming and the American supermarkets play a role in the history of Lean Management. As well as the father of the Toyota production system, Taiichi Ohno. In order to understand the Lean philosophy, a basic understanding of its history is necessary. This will be presented in the upcoming sections.

Flow – Henry Ford

The search for the origins of Lean Management starts with Henry Ford and the Ford Motor Company. Henry Ford has become known through his T-model and mass production (assembly line). Especially his sentence "You can have any kind of colour as long as it's black" characterizes Ford's way of thinking. Henry Ford introduced the assembly line in the auto industry after visiting slaughterhouses in Chicago. In these slaughterhouses the pigs were attached to hooks and are pulled on rails. Henry Ford took this idea and applied it to the car industry. Thus, the slaughterhouses are the predecessors of Henry Ford's assembly line, and at the same time a supplier of ideas for innovation in the production of automobiles.

At the same time, Ford started to use the assembly line and introduced the flow principle, a process which aligns all its individual steps. But to achieve this, Ford needed to overcome another hurdle.

This time, the starting point is the car manufacturing industry itself. In the beginning of automobile production each car was a single piece and therefore not identical. This means that parts did not always fit directly to the body, but had to be adjusted by hand. To solve this problem, Henry Ford introduced the standardized quality, which for the automotive industry nowadays goes without saying.

Gemba – Sakichi Toyoda

Taiichi Ohno described Sakichi Toyoda as an ingenious inventor whose ideas were based solely on his personal performance. He did not study at a university and did not read any professional literature. Instead, he studied the problems and solutions in practice through hours of observation with the sole intention of determining the true cause of a problem, to analyse it and to test the success of his solution. As such, inventions that emerged from practice had a more successful implementation in real-world situations. This principle significantly influenced Toyota and the Toyota Production System and is today known as Genchi Genbutsu.

Jidoka – Kiichiro Toyoda

Kiichiro Toyoda is the son of Sakichi Toyoda, who founded Toyoda Spinning and Weaving Company. This was the beginning of the history of Jidoka and the Toyota Motor Corporation. Sakichi Toyoda continued to develop his father's automatic looms by integrating the **Jidoka** principle. As a result, the loom automatically stops once the thread is finished or is torn. At that time, this was a revolution, since an employee now could operate and monitor several machines instead of one single machine. This drastically improved the quality as well as the productivity of their machines. Jidoka as such is considered as **Automation** and is today implemented in the form of **First Defect Stop** in Lean Management.

Kaizen – Masaaki Imai

Kaizen is **improvement for the better** and it is generally assumed that it finds its origin in Asian culture. In this culture dealing with mistakes and dealing with improvements is different in comparison to the approach of the Western world. For example, when an apprentice copies the Sensei's (Teacher) script and this copy is of a higher quality, it is an honour for both. It is not considered as a copy, and certainly not as a confession of guilt of how badly the master has worked. On the contrary, it leads to a completely different **basis for improvement**. A teacher once said: "In physics, there is only true progress when the old generation has become extinct and a new generation grows up that is familiar with it." Again, the basis for **change = improvement** is different. The author Masaaki Imai contributed significantly to the dissemination of this idea in the West with his book "Kaizen".

Supermarket and Toyota/TPS – Taiichi Ohno

When Taiichi Ohno visited the US to find out about new American manufacturing processes in the automotive industry, he also came into contact with the American supermarket principle. This principle was scarcely known in that time and includes the concept of presence of goods in the sales area, no warehouses and demand-oriented reordering, i.e. ordering according to consumption. Taiichi Ohno and his employees applied this idea to their production in the form of today's kanban (= card), creating what we know as a demand-oriented production. However, the teams around Taiichi Ohno not only used this principle, in contrast to other techniques, as a tool but also developed it as a driving element in Kaizen. Thanks to the ability of Toyota and its employees, this tool has not only been developed but has been integrated into a system and has been designed as a sustainable motor for improvement. Taiichi Ohno, who is a major contributor to the development of the TPS, led the Toyota-team at that time.

Single (Digit) Minute Exchange of Die (SMED) und Poka Yoke – Shigeo Shingo

As part of the development of the Toyota Production System (TPS), Shigeo Shingo is allocated the responsibility of developing a way of systematic set-up time reduction. He is regarded as a pioneer in this field and plays a major role in the implementation of pull systems. These include SMED and error prevention by Poka Yoke, i.e. error prevention systems.

PDCA – William Edwards Deming

William Edwards Deming is referred to as a major contributor to the Japanese corporate culture, which is known to feel strongly about producing the highest quality. After his quality-increasing theories fell on deaf ears in the US, he went east to Japan. The Japanese listened to him and even named one of the most important quality prizes after him, the Deming Prize, which has been awarded in Japan since 1950. His contribution for quality and in particular the dissemination of the PDCA methodology (Plan, Do, Check, Act), which is of particular importance in process optimization, has a major position in any Lean Management System. Deming's approaches fall back on the theories of Walter A. Shewhart.

Ishikawa-Diagram – Kaoru Ishikawa

Kaoru Ishikawa developed the Ishikawa diagram, a cause-and-effect diagram, which is named after him and is now among the seven statistical tools of Lean Management. He also studied group-oriented concepts and is regarded as the inventor of the quality circle, a method which was completely misunderstood and misinterpreted in the West during the 1980s.

Lean Management

James P. Womack, Daniel T. Jones and Daniel Roos are, together with their project leaders John F. Krafcik and John P. MacDuffie, are the inventors of the term "Lean Management". These MIT researchers, who investigated production systems of various car manufacturers within the scope of a research project called International Motor Vehicle Program (IMVP), finally published a benchmark analysis, which is documented in the book "The Machine That Changed the World". The published results show the serious differences between Western and Asian (mainly Japanese) manufacturers and changed the point of view within the entire car industry. They named the principle they observed Lean Management, which is made up of the experience gained from various companies and observations in practice.

Figure 1.1 gives an overview of the Lean history.

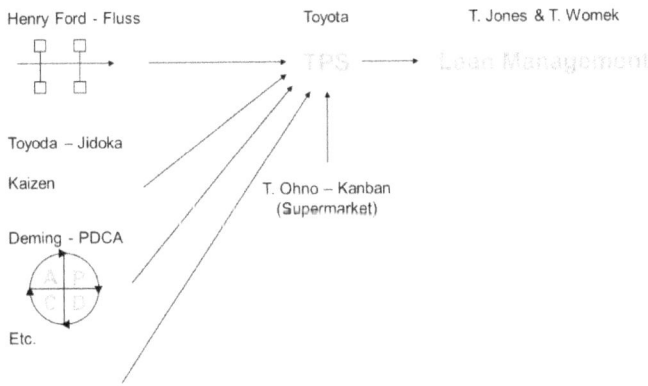

Figure 1.1 Lean history

Lean Six Sigma

Lean Six Sigma is the latest attempt to combine Lean Management and Six Sigma concepts in order to use the best of both. It should be noted that this concept is only at its beginning and still has to prove itself in practice.

The richness of the various lines of thought reflect the history of Lean Management and the true origin and strength of this philosophy. It did not originate in a university or on a drawing board, but was systematically developed by many experts of world rank and tested and refined in practice. The Toyoda family and Taiichi Ohno are essentially responsible for the fact that these different ideas have been brought together under a single roof to form a system and have been consistently implemented. This has allowed the various approaches to develop their full performance and make Toyota Motor Corporation one of the world's largest companies.

The Toyota Production System was characterized by its special conditions during development:

- lack of raw materials (high costs)
- low production quantities with a high number of variants
- capital shortage
- high quality requirements

Today's cut-throat competitions are demanding companies to achieve these special requirements as well, reflecting the timeliness and success of Lean Management and Lean companies, led by Toyota. Toyota began its first deliveries on the American market in 1955. Today, Toyota is one of the world's largest car manufacturers. While the style of leadership usually changes, after a change of leadership in the top line, by emphasizing other targets, Toyota continues its path after Dr. Ing. Deming's motto "constancy of purpose".

2. Guidelines for implementing Lean Management

2.1 Understanding the lean philosophy

If Lean Management is considered to be one of the many management methods commonly used in practice or in textbooks, the following happens in practice: based on methods and instruments documented in specialist books, a quick introduction is made with the expectation that the same success as, e.g. for Toyota or Porsche, will be achieved immediately. If you look at companies that have followed this strategy, you will see a truly lean production at first sight. According to the monthly audit reports, methods like 5S or Zoning are exemplary implemented, and top management is enthusiastic: mission completed.

However, if you look behind the scenes, little has changed in these companies. The attitude of the employees towards continuous improvement or the attitude of the managers towards errors and problems is still the same. Improvements have emerged, the efficiency of some processes has undoubtedly improved, but there can be no question of a "resounding" success. We are dealing here with the variant "Lean Window Dressing". The external appearance (the visible elements of Lean) are pointing to lean management, but from a real implementation one is still light years away (implementation of the non-visible elements of Lean Management).

Reduction of changeover times by using SMED

The changeover time reduction of machines and systems by SMED (Single Minute Exchange of Die; see chapter 7) can be implemented as a single measure. This reduces production costs and throughput times. The efficacy of this measure, however, evaporates completely and often leads to even greater inventories if no integration into the entire value stream of production takes place.

How can this objective state of real Lean Management be achieved? The following answers to this question are helpful:

- Lean Management must be understood as a business philosophy, not as a method. Philosophy means that the lean principles are understood and supported by all employees. This process starts at the top level. If Lean Management is not sustained and intensified by the top management, success will not occur.
- The methods, instruments and tools of Lean Management are only a means of bringing the company (step-by-step) closer to the vision. These are never a goal on their own, but are used as required and adapted to the specific tasks for problem solving.
- Implementing the Lean Management philosophy at a company begins with the employees and their attitude towards errors, problems, improvements, elimination of waste and their focus on product value or service towards the customer. This requires a cultural change that cannot be achieved within a few months. If this appears to be too time-intensive and too complex for the management, only the window dressing of the term will remain.

The core of Lean Management can be described by five principles (see Womack 2003):

- *Specify the value of the product or service:* The value of a product or service is determined exclusively by the customer. For this reason, the requirements of the customer and their "appreciation" of products and services

or their operations are the first priority for companies that want to implement Lean Management.
- *Identify the value stream of the product or service:* This is not only about the internal supply chain, but the whole network of companies (suppliers, suppliers of suppliers, etc.) responsible for the production of a finished good (external supply chain). All activities (whether creating value or not) are part of the value stream and are therefore the subject of the production and / or process system (Lean Management).
- *Value flow without interruption:* this lean principle calls for a value-added process, which is not interrupted by the storage of (half-)finished products and by storage times in the production process. This principle is most difficult to implement, since the stacking of intermediate steps (batch production) seems to be a kind of natural law of human functioning, which is reluctantly replaced by the flow principle.
- *Pull the value by the customer:* According to this principle, the value stream is not initiated by the planning process of the manufacturing company, but by the requirement or the demand of the (end) customer. It is therefore only produced when the products or the services are needed.
- *Strive for perfection:* Just as learning in our knowledge society never ceases, Kaizen (Lean Management) is a permanent task. The implementation of the flow and pull principle can always be improved. Even companies like Toyota, which have started Kaizen (Lean Management) more than 50 years ago, are still striving for perfection.

2.2 Added Value

If we want to know the definition of value, one can use the question "What does the customer want?" Here, the distinction is made between processes that the customer "wants" and processes that the customer does not "want". This is the description of added value and waste (Muda). Added value is exclusively about value-adding activities/process steps that are of benefit to the customer and which he is willing to pay a higher price for.

Added Value: handles are attached on a crate, which enable the customer to carry it easier.

2.3 Waste, unevenness, overburden

Waste is the sand in the enterprise transmission, which leads to high costs, inadequate efficiency and lack of effectiveness in the achievement of its goals. Therefore, elimination of waste is one of the core objectives of Lean Management. But Lean Management goes even further. An overview of the Lean Management objectives:

- Avoidance of waste (*Muda*),
- Elimination of unevenness (*Mura*),
- Reduction of overburden (*Muri*).

Waste (in the Japanese language referred to as *Muda*) is a key concept in Lean Management. This means any activity that consumes resources in any form (labour hours, space, machines, etc.) but does not generate any value.

Waste is found in all areas of life. Not only in a company's production department, but as well in service companies, public administration and company warehouses.

Lean Management is an efficient weapon against waste because it shows how to recognize and organize value-adding activities in such a way that all of the following forms of waste are largely eliminated:

- Overproduction: production of products for which there are no orders, resulting in additional stock
- Waiting time: employees who are waiting for the completion of a previous process step and have no work due to an error or due to technical failures and capacity bottlenecks
- Unnecessary transport or delivery: transport of semi-finished products over long distances, transport of material into or from a warehouse or between process steps
- Unnecessary or incorrect processes: inefficient processes due to poor tools or product design as well as unnecessary process steps
- Excess inventories: unnecessary stocks of semi-finished products and finished products or the storing of obsolete parts or products
- Unnecessary movement: unnecessary movement or activities of employees during a production step (for example, bringing tools and materials, picking up and moving a workpiece over and over again)
- Defects: production of faulty parts (rejects) or error recovery (rework)
- Unused creativity of employees: loss of time, ideas, potential for improvement, skills and opportunities to learn when employees are not involved in the improvement process

Unevenness (*Mura*) is caused by an insufficient adjustment/levelling of production resource capacities in the supply chain and employees in production. Symptoms are storage of semi-finished products in workshops or at work stations. This is often due to a poor central production planning and control system which is not able to guarantee a non-interrupted value stream.

Self-regulating control circuits (*Kanban*) or timely, on-demand delivery of parts (just-in-time) are a good means of eliminating *Mura*.

Overburden (*Muri*) in the production process occurs when employees are overburdened by the predefined workload (for example, incorrect default times) or ergonomically unfavourable workstations. This also applies to machines and systems resulting in material queues in front of the overloaded workstations, machine downtimes and errors in the execution of work procedures. In addition, employees' work satisfaction is impaired and therefore the value stream is being disrupted.

Overuse is also caused by the overburden of employees due to confusing jobs and intransparent processes. Not being challenged enough, on the other hand, leads to negligence.

2.4 Value added curve

One of the main basic principles of Lean Management is the visualization of problems and deficits during operation. This enables the management to make the "dimension" of the respective problem visible and thus support the decision-making process.

The value-added curve is a new tool in Lean Management and is suitable for visualizing the extent of waste (see Pautsch 2010). In the English-speaking world, this instrument has already long been used under the name of "Cost-time Profile" and is being used as a standard tool within the framework of logistics controlling.

When using this tool in Lean Management, the respective value of the product is cumulated during the manufacturing process and divided into three categories based on an analysis (e.g. value stream analysis):

- *Value creation* shows the actual benefits of the respective production step. This is viewed by the customer as a contribution to the value of the product.
- *Waste Type I* is an activity which does not represent a contribution to the customer product value. Due to technical or other circumstances, elimination of this type of waste is not yet possible, but step by step it can be reduced.
- *Waste type II* is also not considered by the customer as a contribution to the product value. The realization of Lean Management, organizational and technical possibilities that can be implemented today can be used to eliminate this type of waste.

Figure 2.1 shows a value added curve. The value of the considered product increases with each process step towards completion. The accompanying waste can be represented in the value-growth curve as a unit of value (difference of the integral beneath the curves) and thus a visual impression of the extent of waste takes place. This demonstrates the potential that can be achieved through realization of a Lean initiative.

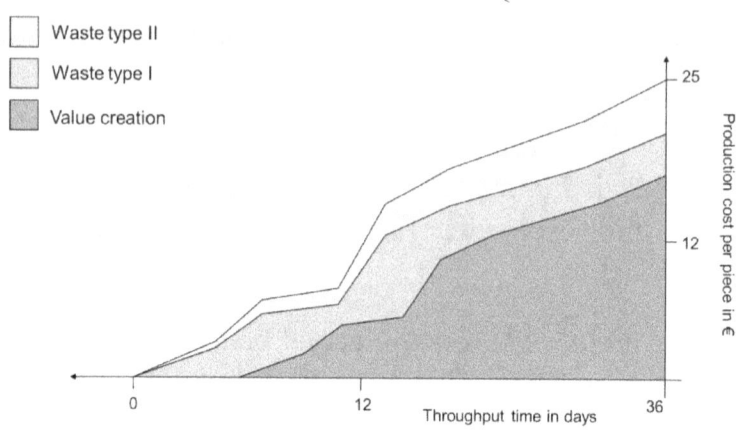

Figure 2.1 Value added curve

2.5 Implementation

Each Lean project is different, which is why only general comments for implementation can be presented here. Based on practice-oriented experiences (Drew/McCallum/Roggenhofer 2005), a successful implementation could cover seven steps:

Unrestricted will of the company's management to introduce Lean Management and to unconditionally support the implementation process.

This first step is the most important. Without the "backbone" of management, Lean Management cannot be introduced into the corporate reality. Even more problematic is that the introduction of Lean Management is an "all or nothing" decision. A "little lean" is just as impossible as a "little pregnant". Lean management requires the full support, especially when the initial difficulties in employee acceptance occur and initial setbacks (which are often unavoidable) happen.

Decisive as well is that all employees of the company recognize that Lean is not an alibi for draconian cost reduction programs to ultimately reach a mass lay-off. If this is the case, Lean will not be successful and will be stuck in the first stages of implementation.

The implementation process has to be supported by experienced Lean experts.

Reading professional literature and training employees in Lean Management are no doubt helpful. However, Lean Management requires such a radical rethinking that the support of experts who bring hands-on experience from companies that successfully implemented Lean Management is necessary. These can be consultants, but also employees from companies that have already implemented Lean Management.

The advantage of these lean experts is that they have practice experience and, moreover, knowledge of the hurdles that may present themselves during the implementation process. Lean management often requires employees to give up on strategies which were once considered to be important for the survival of the company. This may be, for example, a safety stock of key components for production, all of which are to be dismantled as part of Lean Management. Resistance is to be expected here. It is the experienced Lean expert who is able to moderate and navigate this necessary learning process.

The operational objectives of the management have to be aligned with the Lean objectives.

At the beginning of each Lean project, there are company objectives, which must be viewed in the light of the Lean philosophy. If a clear decision is made for Lean Management, each of these goals has to be checked on their compatibility with the lean initiatives. In principle, Lean objectives must be prioritized.

Identification of improvement potential.

Based on an actual analysis of the company processes, we explore the possibilities for waste elimination and different points of imbalance in the value stream. The value stream, one could also say "material flow" in a very simplistic manner, ideally runs as on a conveyor belt. A current that flows at the same speed until the product arrives at the customer's end. The value flow does not accumulate at any point (there are no dams: stockpiles with long periods). However, the current is not accelerated anywhere neither (there is no waterfall: point acceleration by fast machines or express freight). Waterfalls and dams cost extra money, are indeed waste and should therefore be eliminated.

Defining the ideal state.

After waste, unevenness and overburden are recognized, the desired ideal state can be described. This is often documented as a vision and a management commitment to implement it according to a defined schedule.

Implementation of a pilot project.

Anyone who has experienced the introduction of a new ERP software in the form of a big bang in his or her company knows the problem of total chaos, triggered by the premature and complete introduction of new concepts. Therefore, a careful implementation in the form of a pilot project is advisable in Lean Management. The advantages of a pilot project are convincing: we can demonstrate employees in a real-life environment that Lean functions and which benefits are possible. This also, in turn, motivates further projects. In addition, the management does not impose any risk to the company's existence if there are setbacks. In addition, when difficulties occur corrections to the concepts are easier to facilitate.

Implementation of Lean Management across the entire company.

Lean Management is implemented throughout the company following the success of the pilot project. The implementation of Lean concepts throughout the company is not the end of the story. The pursuit of perfection requires a constant development of Lean Management. Within the framework of the continuous improvement process, the company processes are constantly being expanded an built upon to achieve this goal.

Toyota has over 50 years of experience with Lean methods. If you ask a Toyota manager about the current state of implementation or when the process of improvement will be completed, he or she would be confused by the question. Just as perfection is never achieved, the process of continuous improvement is never completed. When implementing Lean Management, it is always important to consider that it is not a method such as statistical process regulation, but a company philosophy, which must be internalized and supported by all employees. It is precisely this invisible component of Lean Management which makes a decisive contribution to the success of the project and is undoubtedly the greater hurdle in the realization compared to, say, implementing a Kanban system. This may be the reason why many companies are neglecting the non-visible part. Consequently, the achieved successes in these cases will fall short of expectations.

3. Kaizen – Continuous Improvement (CI)

The term *Kaizen* comes from Japanese and means **change for the better** (Kai = improvement, zen = good). The English equivalent of this is continuous improvement, which never ends and is thus seen as the pursuit for **perfection**.

The basic principle of continuous improvement is that of an infinite sequence of small steps on a staircase. Innovation, on the other hand, is aimed at large jumps, which are, however, related to each other at considerable intervals.

Compared to the classic company philosophy, Lean companies do not escape any of these approaches. In particular, since innovation has the property of losing efficiency without constant improvement over time and therefore does not reach its full potential (Figure 3.1).

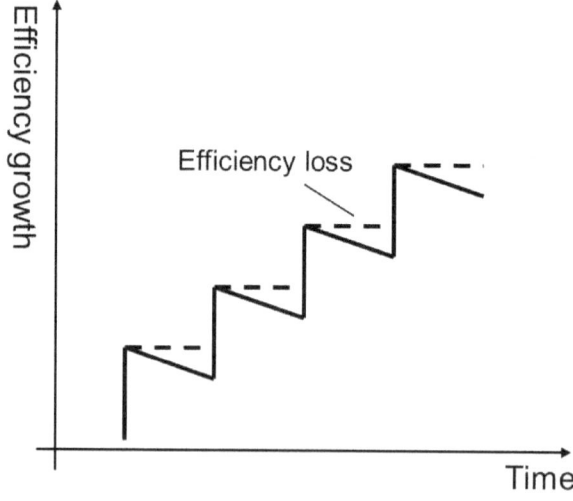

Figure 3.1 Efficiency loss

Lean companies take this into account and use both innovation and Kaizen. This results in much higher efficiency in operational implementation (Figure 3.2). Innovation is understood as the organizational and technical change (resulting from both research and capital use).

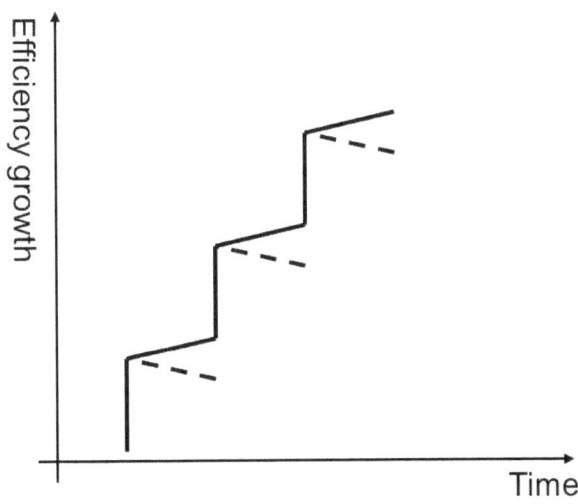

Figure 3.2 Innovation and Kaizen

With the Kaizen philosophy, one tries not to stand still (keep the engine running, so to speak) and to use the creativity of all employees in order to gain an advantage over competitors. This requires ...

... the sustainable implementation of Kaizen and at the same time represents a huge challenge for the organization:
- Kaizen cannot be delegated and dictated
- no system, no structure, no kaizen
- no capacities, no kaizen
- Kaizen is 100% dependent on people
- Kaizen knows no compromises
- no defect culture, no kaizen (see chapter 3.1)

The realization of Kaizen in a company requires some prerequisites:
- Hansei – need of self-reflection
- Hoshin Kanri – Policy Deployment
- Genchi Genbutsu and Gemba
- lean structure/objectives
- individual improvements
- workshops/teamwork
- internal suggestion scheme

3.1 Hansei – Necessity of self-reflection

WHAT IS IT ALL ABOUT?

One cannot see and know everything. Unfortunately we forget this all too often, especially in the professional world. We are often of the opinion that admitting an error is equivalent to that of one's failure. An organization, however, who wants to live Kaizen has to create the preconditions for an environment in which mistakes are not seen as a failure, but as an opportunity for improvement. Then, error occurrence or a deviation from the plan is the prerequisite for improvement (Figure 3.3).

The improvement in itself requires the necessity. Without the need for improvement, there is no Kaizen. This, in turn, means that everything that one does or creates is not perfect or complete and must therefore be changed. This in turn means that there cannot be improvement without change.

Without the understanding of the culture of mistakes, performing Kaizen is not possible.

Figure 3.3 Self-reflection (The personal self-assessment differs from the real one, therefore we use the mirror image to get a feedback.)

WHY SHOULD WE DO THIS?

Kaizen makes it possible to open the door to a higher efficiency and profitability and to go the needed distance. Technical problems at production units can now be solved, since these are not regarded as given. Everything is questioned and taken under consideration for improvement. The political hurdles are resolved and the power of the employees is strengthened. Everyone is now asked to realistically assess their own mistakes as well as reveal thcm to the larger team.

The typical utilization runs through the entire company and all lean tools, which represent the AS IS-state and question it. Examples are:
- Genchi Genbutsu and Gemba (see chapter 3.3)
- Kaizen workshops (see chapter 3.6)
- Poka Yoke (see chapter 8)
- etc.

3.2 Hoshin Kanri – Policy Deployment

WHAT IS IT ALL ABOUT?

Under *Hoshin Kanri*/Policy Deployment, we understand the strategic orientation of the company and the Lean system. It is thus the integration of long-, medium- and short-term goals into the Lean system. The special feature of *Hoshin Kanri* is the agreement between the top and lower levels. This means that the objectives are presented in detail, both vertically and horizontally, to the level of the individual machines, and thus a shared target agreement is formed. Lean thereby creates management space as well as the need for improvement whilst simultaneously solving it. The planning of Kaizen is a significant contribution to Kaizen itself. Starting from following objectives:

- abstract objectives – company vision
- specific objectives – annual budgets
- operational objectives – OEE (Overall Equipment Effectiveness)
- corporate objectives – production line-OEE
- personalized targets – machine-OEE, etc.

The aim is to show every employee what his contribution to the fulfilment of the overall company objective is at a level which is understandable and operationally viable for him (Figure 3.4).

Figure 3.4 Hoshin Kanri employee level

Furthermore, the objectives are to be geared towards improvement. This means that already improved and stabilized areas are removed from the first level of target positioning and the areas that are to be improved move forward.

WHY SHOULD WE DO THIS?

By using Hoshin Kanri we achieve that each employee is bound to the company strategy and is informed about the background and goals. Employees can participate in the goal setting process and thus influence the allocation of unrealistic goals, as well as align them with the improvement of processes. They are more motivated and keep the objective in mind, which leads to more bundled actions in the company. As such Lean Management produces a higher degree of target achievement than conventional target methods and generates a higher economic success.

3.3 Genchi Genbutsu and Gemba

WHAT IS IT ALL ABOUT?

Genchi Genbutsu is a Japanese term that aims to "go and convince yourself". The term includes the concept of *Gemba*: "Go to the place where it happens and do not try to guess the solution from the office." Moreover, *Genchi Genbutsu* also includes:
- The place of action
- Watch what happens with your own eyes
- Compare good parts with bad parts
- Take a look at the real problems at the location where they arise

WHY SHOULD WE DO THIS?

Contact with reality is of great importance for improvement. Genchi Genbutsu commits itself to confrontation with real data and self-observation on-site, it thus forces to keep aloof from assumptions and decisions without a real basis.

During a SMED-Kaizen workshop, the group of employees (after the theoretical introduction) begins to understand the problem, e.g. by answering 7M (see chapter 12). This is done by partially moderating the workshop next to the machine. The data are then collected and checked.

This is followed by the observation of the changeover process during normal production operations. Beforehand, the team does not make assumptions about the sequence or individual time of the changeover steps.

3.4 Lean structure/objectives

WHAT IS IT ALL ABOUT?

A further aspect of improvement for the better, i.e. *Kaizen*, is the structure required for this. There are three essential aspects to consider. First, it is important to create the resources. Secondly, the organization must be shaped. Lastly, it is necessary to communicate the objectives and the corresponding data. These are generated within the framework of the *Hoshin Kanri*/Policy Deployment, but must be mediated and implemented or enforced. Lean Management uses the following two Lean tools: visual management and team structure. For Visual Management, we refer to chapter 4.

The Lean team structure assumes that employees must be led to generate *Kaizen*.

Another important aspect of implementing Lean Management is the introduction of APUs (Autonomous Production Units) to ensure the necessary resources.

WHY SHOULD WE DO THIS?

In addition to visual management, the team structure is a Lean tool to convert the goal and motivation of employees into Kaizen. This structure also provides resources.

For one or more manufacturing zones, there is a team consisting of employees and one team leader. The team leader works at least 50% in production, the remainder of his time is devoted to support and the coordination of the team and to fulfil his own *Kaizen* tasks. The team leader is not a supervisor/manager.

A team leader has 5 ± 2 employees to lead. The next level is the supervisor. He leads 5 ± 2 team leaders and works in a management function. That means he takes part in management routines and trains employees. The APU manager is positioned above the supervisor, who also manages 5 ± 2 employees (Figure 3.5).

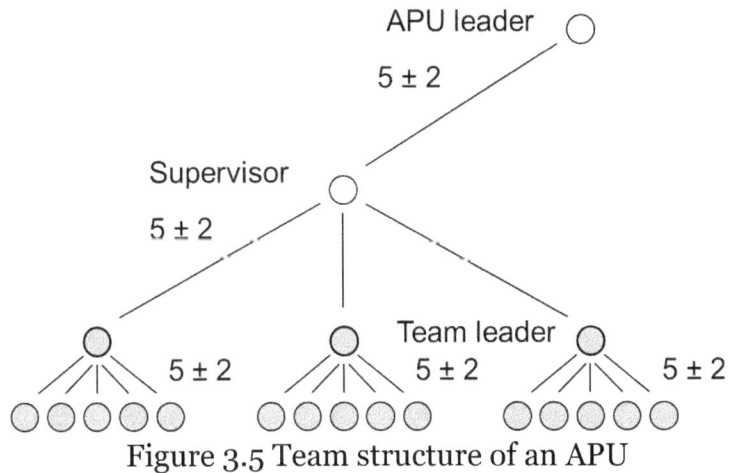

Figure 3.5 Team structure of an APU

3.5 Individual improvements

WHAT IS IT ALL ABOUT?

Lean management generates individual improvement starting from the motivation of employees. Specifically, it is an improvement of an employee, which he has developed himself and which is ready to be made operational. The drivers are the target, the team structure and the competence to be able to initiate improvements (see chapter 3.7).

WHY SHOULD WE DO THIS?

This means that there are initiatives/programs that give the individual the opportunity to introduce any kind of improvement. The organization must follow the improvements and implement them when and where they are meaningful. Thus, in addition to the monetary objectives, the organization or company is forced to promote active improvement and to anchor it as a main target in its company policy. This, of course, eventually leads to a higher economic performance.

The team leader of a production cell asks his team, but also every individual, to improve in order to achieve our goals. The employees meet and discuss problem A and B. They use Lean tools, e.g. brainstorming, and work out a solution. Individual solutions and ideas are always introduced during this process.

The results and findings are presented to the team leader. He accepts the approach and starts, together with his team, the implementation and in-practice tests.

3.6 Workshops/teamwork

WHAT IS IT ALL ABOUT?

Lean Management lives from constant and sustainable improvement. Both individual and group-specific improvements are used for this purpose. If this improvement cannot be achieved through everyday work, Lean Management will rely on *Kaizen* workshops.

These *Kaizen* workshops focus on specific problem areas. *Kaizen* workshops usually last three to four days and involve various members of the company. Here, both specialists as well as employees of unrelated departments are asked to develop a solution for the problem. These types of workshops follow the PDCA cycle and have a clear target.

The management takes part in these *Kaizen* workshops. However, this may be limited to certain parts of it.

At the end of the workshop, the results will be presented to the management as well as the department in order to communicate the gathered knowledge and to put it into practice in the next product generation.

WHY SHOULD WE DO THIS?

On the one hand , the use of topic-specific *Kaizen* workshops makes it possible to deal with complex problems. On the other hand, the company or management signals the importance of the improvement towards its employees. The special importance of *Kaizen* becomes particularly visible by releasing the necessary resources, as well as forcing the workshop participants to find solutions in a quick and cost-effective manner. By providing the resources, the management signals the importance of the task set-up as well as the support of the employees, thus increasing motivation.

The change-over time at the injection unit is over two hours. This represents a problem, as customers expect greater flexibility. The APU leader has requested a team to do a SMED workshop.

1. The workshop starts with the goal of its management: In this case, cut the set-up time by half.
2. The Lean Manager begins with introducing the theory and Lean tools.
3. This is followed by Gemba, i.e. the gathering of information and data at the machine and during the process.
4. Next, the changeover process is monitored. It is important that this is a normal changeover. In this case, data such as time, distance and responsibility as well as general findings are collected.
5. The evaluation of the changeover process is carried out. The team discusses the data and observations with the changeover team. A new set-up sequence is now generated with consideration of the Lean tools. If possible, improvements are immediately implemented by the team.
6. Now Gemba is on the agenda again! The new set-up sequence is an assumption without any further test, says the Lean Manager, so the team does another changeover and observes this in the same way as the first time.
7. Improvements are detected and the new set-up process as well as the new target time are determined. The teams determine when employees are to be trained and an action plan is created.
8. This is followed by a presentation for the management in which the results are presented and further steps for sustainability are defined.

3.7 Internal suggestion scheme

WHAT IS IT ALL ABOUT?

Lean Management not only focuses on targeted improvement, which is generated by the tools described, but also on self-motivation of its employees. For this, Lean Management pursues a principle whereby every employee has the right to submit an improvement. This right is not limited to its work environment, but is allowed to be part of the improvement in any business process. The claim to improvement gives the employee the right to insist on a response to the proposal as well as a positive evaluation on an implementation within a short period of time, including the award.

WHY SHOULD WE DO THIS?

Lean Management pursues the goal of promoting creativity of the employee and the possibility of using Kaizen. In addition, the internal improvement allows to reduce operational blindness and gives new ideas' full scope. Employees with a stronger self-motivation than others are therefore integrated into the improvement process and thus motivated. The employee is not to be left alone by the management but is to be strengthened in its improvement initiatives.

If employees submit suggestions for improvement, they should be answered within 24/48 hours. This leads to a higher motivation for the employee, since he receives feedback and is thus sure that he is being heard. In other words, long response times lead to demotivation!

A machine operator has been annoyed for months about the constant failure of a packaging unit (a daily occurrence in many companies!). This issue is initially caused by the deformation of a cardboard box, which resulted from the changing weather conditions (humidity). The employee develops an idea by which the cardboard can be guided better during the packaging process. After the successful test and presentation, this system is defined as a standard and, in this case, the employee is rewarded with a bonus.

4. Visual management – learning to see

Information transfer is one of the most important tasks in today's society. If we transfer this problem onto companies, one faces the same challenges as in society. Quantity is not equal to quality. The qualitative decision depends on the quality of the information transfer. The success of a company results from the quality of the decisions and shows us the importance of the information transfer.

Visual Management forms the basis and is an everyday tool for management and employees in a Lean company. It is the foundation for *Kaizen* and Quick Response, the fast response to deviations. It reflects the state of a process, a department or a company in the form of immediately visible information, the target state and the actual state as well as its deviations. The information transfer is carried out directly from and with orientation towards the process, which must lead to immediate action by the responsible persons. It requires and promotes *Kaizen*.

4.1 Value Stream Mapping (VSM)

WHAT IS IT ALL ABOUT?

VSM - value stream mapping is the analysis of a value stream (Figure 4.1). The flow of material and information is represented along the process chain, with the analysis starting from the customer until our suppliers. The individual process steps are recorded and evaluated according to their status, value-increasing or non-value-increasing.

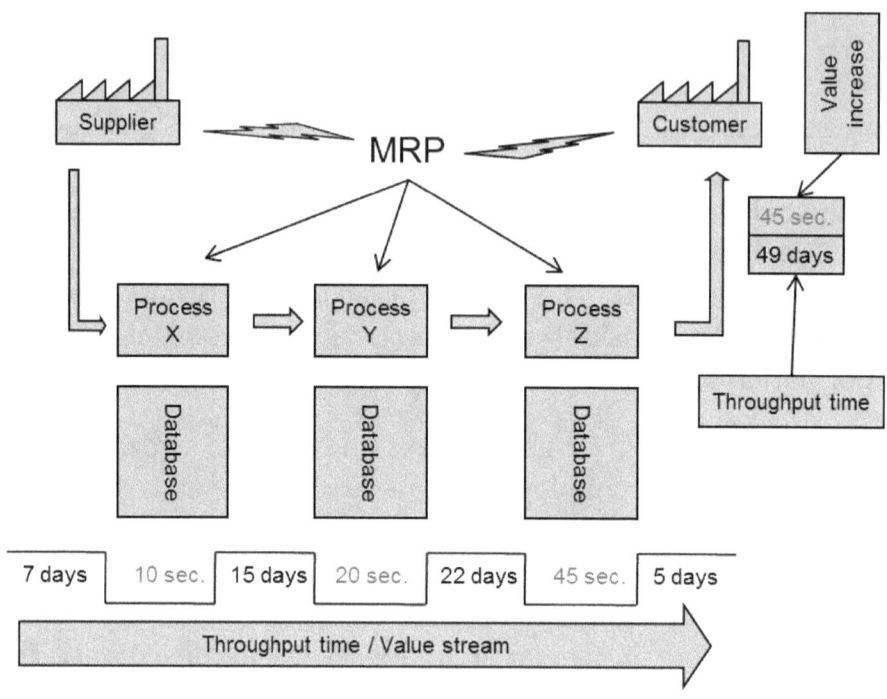

Figure 4.1 Value stream analysis

WHY SHOULD WE DO THIS?

Value stream analysis allows employees and management in a Lean environment to examine the processes from the point of view of the customer and to search for *Muda* (waste). Each individual process step is now examined, evaluated and passed on to its decision. With value stream mapping, Lean Management aims at "seeing" and "learning to see", in other words, the goal is to have the ability to differentiate between value-adding and non-value-adding processes.

For the main processes, detailed data, such as overall equipment effectiveness (OEE), cycle, tact time, etc. For the secondary process the collected data is limited to general process information, times and personnel expenditure. This is done in teamwork and by using *Gemba*. This means that the team goes through the entire process chain from the delivery of the product until delivery of the finished product on site and collects and checks all data directly. This data is now assembled in a meeting room on a large paper according to the VSM rules. As a result of the value stream analysis, an overview of the processes is generated, divided into value-adding and non-value-adding processes, as well as the comparison of the total lead time with the value-adding time.

Experience shows that the discrepancy between the lead time and the value-adding time at the beginning of the Lean effort is astronomically high. In the illustrated example, this is as follows:

$$\frac{value - adding\ time}{lead\ time} = \frac{65.4\ seconds}{58\ days}$$

It is particularly worth mentioning that, in practice, the customer is only willing to pay for the value-adding time!

The team then starts to question individual processes and to derive actions with the aim of reducing the lead time. This can be done using individual *Kaizen* activities or *Kaizen* workshops.

4.2 Key Performance Indicators (KPI)

WHAT IS IT ALL ABOUT?

Imagine driving a car and not having a tachometer. You can only follow the prescribed driving speed "by feeling". It is generally known that the design of the road area and of the vehicle significantly influence the "felt" speed. This means you can only approximately keep the prescribed speed.

Directing a company "based on feeling" is no less dangerous. Following principle applies: "If you can't measure it, you can't manage it." Therefore, key figures are one of the footholds of

Lean Management. However, this does not require a large number of key figures, even if the manufacturers of enterprise resource planning systems want us to believe so. Few, well-selected key figures are sufficient to provide a powerful tool for Visual Management.

How many key figures does a company need?

A large number of key figures obscure what is essential. Few, well-chosen key figures, which are based on the current goals and "focal points" of the company, are sufficient to lead a company. The Lean principle applies not only to processes and strategies, but also to key figures.

WHY SHOULD WE DO THIS?

In the following, two key figures, the Overall Equipment Effectiveness (OEE) and the Total Effective Equipment Productivity (TEEP) are presented. These two key figures are the prerequisite, e.g. for the realization of lean concepts such as Total Productive Maintenance (see chapter 6) or the introduction of continuous improvement processes (see chapter 3).

There are hidden productivity reserves in every production process. The first step is to make them visible.

The performance of a production system is determined by three factors:
- Availability
- Quality
- Performance

Only when all three aspects of the effective performance of production machines are made visible, an improvement in the performance can be started.

Using the example of a sorting system of a packet service, the calculation of OEE is shown. The availability rate is calculated according to the following formula:
Availability rate = (planned production time – unplanned downtime) : planned production time * 100

Availability of the sorting system of a package service
Two shift operation of each eight hours
planned downtime for setup work: ten minutes
Unplanned downtime due to technical problems: 30 minutes
Availability rate =
(969 min - 10 min - 30 min): 950 min. * 100 = 96.8%
(960 - 10 - 30): 950 * 100 = 96.8%

Quality rate = (transported parcels – incorrect assorted parcels) : transported parcels * 100

Quality of the sorting system of a package service
Total number of packages: 60 pieces
Incorrectly sorted packages (manual rework required): 4 pieces
Quality rate = (60 pcs. - 4 pcs.): 60 pcs. * 100 = 93.3%

Performance index = ideal transport time * number of transported parcels : operating time * 100

Performance of the sorting system of a package service
Two shift operation of each eight hours
ideal transport time in the machine: 13 minutes
transported packages: 60 pieces
Power rate = 13 min. * 60 pcs. : 920 min. * 100 = 84.8%

Overall Equipment Effectiveness (OEE) = Availability rate * Quality rate * Performance index

Overall Equipment Effectiveness of the sorting system of a package service
Overall Equipment Effectiveness = 0.968 * 0.848 * 0.933 * 100 = 76.6%

The calculation shows that, despite the fact that the sorting facility (96.8%) seems to have a high availability at first glance, the overall equipment effectiveness is much lower (76.6%). Many companies have an overall equipment effectiveness of less than 60%. With Total Productive Maintenance (see chapter 6) this value can be significantly improved.

The Total Effective Equipment Performance combines the overall equipment effectiveness with the company's planning periods (for example, 24 hours or 365 days in one work year). This shows potentials that go beyond the current horizon of capacity considerations. These "hidden" capacities can then be developed and extended periods of use of the production plants can be considered.

Total Effective Equipment Performance of the sorting system of a package service
Two-shift operation of each eight hours, six days per week
Planning period seven days / 24 hours
Machine load = 8 hours * 2 shifts * 6 days: (7 days * 24 hours) * 100 = 57.14%
Total Effective Equipment Performance (TEEP) = 0.5714 * 0.766 * 100 = 43.77%

A value of 76.6% for the OEE is an acceptable value for a continuous process, but improvements in the direction of 85% are quite possible. In a batch-sized production one could speak of a very good efficiency, improvements in the direction of 80% are possible. Values below 65% indicate a high degree of waste.

The Total Effective Equipment Performance indicator points to possible, still usable capacities and indicates the actual utilization rate of a system.

4.3 Zoning and Andon

Zoning and Andon have an important contribution to the implementation of standards and Visual Management in the production environment.

WHAT IS IT ALL ABOUT?

Zoning is the mapping of a standardized destination of a moving object (Figure 4.2). It is the implementation of the second S of 5S (see chapter 6.3), Seiton, each part has a place and each part is in its place.

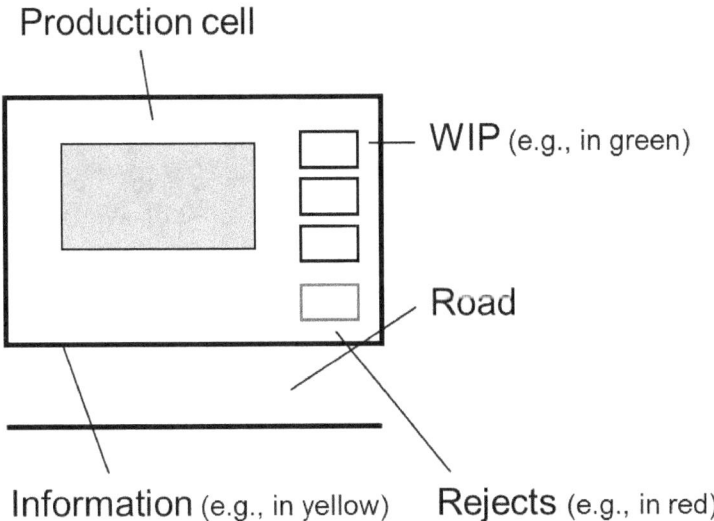

Figure 4.2 Zoning of a production cell

WHY SHOULD WE DO THIS?

Zoning is found in most companies in the form of coloured markings on the floor, such as indicating the place for pallets. This results in visualization and immediate information transfer. For the employee, it is immediately apparent where this pallet belongs. For the supervisor, the so-called feedback is generated as to whether the process is in the standard frame or not.

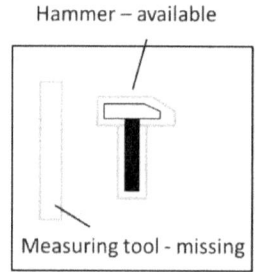

Figure 4.3 Shadow board

Within the framework of a workshop a standardized production cell was defined by the team. The production-specific, as well as the logistic requirements, were taken into account and integrated. In order to standardize this, the team begins to define the areas and mark them with different bands on the ground. The colours red, green and yellow are used to distinguish scrap, materials and information areas (Fig. 4.2). Another example of zoning is the so-called "shadow board". For example, every tool is displayed on the background of a board. The background will be developed within a 5S workshop by the employees by defining the appropriate places for the necessary tools. Afterwards the tools are drawn from the model onto the board. This allows the employee to straightaway identify which tool belongs to which location. It is much more important, however, that the employee can straightaway check the board for its completeness. This can, for example, prevent the changeover time of a machine becoming unnecessarily prolonged by a missing tool (Fig. 4.3).

WHAT IS IT ALL ABOUT?

Andon is the visual representation of the current status of the production equipment in a production environment (Fig. 4.4). Andon forms this current status with various light-emitting diodes or light tubes and immediately signals to the user whether or not the production is in progress. The signalling is affected by means of colours: e.g. green for production, red for breakdown, or by produced parts displayed on an electronic board.

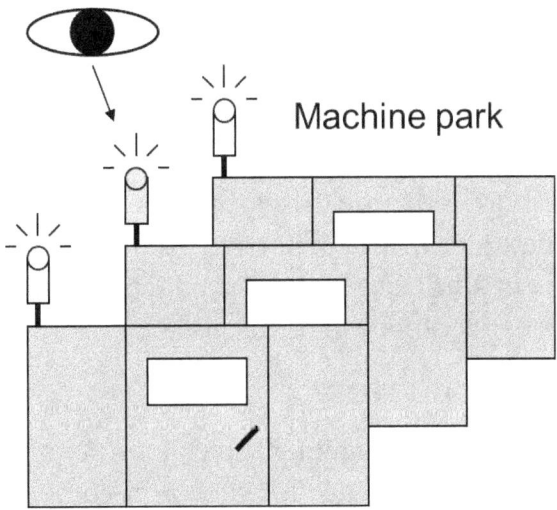

Figure 4.4 Andon in a production area

WHY SHOULD WE DO THIS?

The resulting advantage is that both employees and management are able to recognize the current state of production. This allows immediate action or measures to be taken to counteract a process deviation. These are thus management tools which help to develop Lean Management routines and therefore enable Lean to actively live day-in and day-out throughout the year.

The team (shift leader, team leader and machine operator) is always informed about the status of the machine by installing the light signals and its connection to the machine (Fig. 4.4).

4.4 Jidoka/First Defect Stop

WHAT IS IT ALL ABOUT?

First Defect Stop is the modern way of implementing the idea of *Jidoka*. In this concept, a production unit is provided with a fully automatic stop as soon as an error is detected. The employee has to take care of the defective part, i.e. to solve the quality problem within a given time (for example within one cycle). If the employee is not able to correct the error within the specified time, he/she has to contact the next supervisor level. The supervisor now supports his co-worker during troubleshooting. If the fault cannot be remedied by both, the next supervisor decides whether the short-term measures that have just been taken to protect the customer from a defective production or whether the measures are not sufficient and the production has to be stopped. After this, further actions will be discussed.

WHY SHOULD WE DO THIS?

With *Jidoka*, Lean Management has 100% of its attention devoted to quality. Each cause for each non-compliant part must be examined and eliminated. There is a clear approach, which leaves the employee not alone with the problem at the machine, but also provides further escalation stages. With the increasing stops of the production line, Lean Management forces the organization to solve these problems.

A fully automatic unit is stopped as soon as an error is detected and immediately signals this. The machine operator goes to the faulty part and starts the analysis as described above. The prerequisite for this case (fully automatic unit) is that it has a machine control system which is capable of carrying out this operation.

4.5 Goal and current status

WHAT IS IT ALL ABOUT?

Lean Management tries to trigger *Kaizen* by setting goals and pushing them into the organization. *Hoshin Kanri*/Policy Deployment and team structure are the two tools next to Visual Management. Now, systems are used to communicate and visualize the goal and degree of achievement or the deviation immediately in the factory. The focus of the objective is on continuous improvement.

WHY SHOULD WE DO THIS?

This means that the company's objectives are announced and operationalized and deviations are communicated to every employee. For this purpose, documents are developed that allow the employee to view, compare and recognize the deviation at a glance, the goal and the current performance status. This leads to possibilities for decision-making and the need for the latter, since the specification and the deviation are signalled. This applies to both the employee and the management. Management and specialists in the company are now inadvertently forced to practice *Gemba*!

A number of documents are now used at the production unit. These documents are maintained by the employees themselves and evaluated together with the management (Figure 4.5).

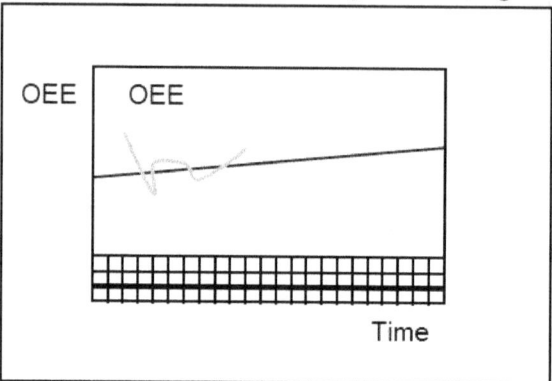

Figure 4.5 OEE document at the machine

The employees record the waste, the production quantity, the Overall Equipment Effectiveness (OEE) and the Total Effective Equipment Productivity (TEEP). Since the introduction of the documents, the production meeting has been moved from the meeting room to the shop floor. The OEE survey shows a negative trend. The team discusses, within the framework of the daily production meeting, about the reasons derived from the Pareto diagram, which was previously prepared based on a trend development. On this basis, a problem becomes apparent at the station, which could not be solved so far. This problem has existed for years, but was not explicitly visible without recording. The APU manager is now confronted by the team with this result and countermeasures are discussed with him.

5. Pull principle

WHAT IS IT ALL ABOUT?

Pull stands for the implementation of the *Kanban* philosophy in a holistic concept. Contrary to the general MRP-II (Manufacturing Resource Planning) philosophy, production is being 'pulled' instead of pushed. It is a demand-oriented fabrication which produces only when the consumer, for instance when a customer or an upstream production unit, asks for a product. *Kanban*, which moves within a control loop and determines the maximum stock in the control loop, is used to transfer the production-triggering information.

WHY SHOULD WE DO THIS?

By concentrating on Pull, in combination with the *Muda* philosophy, Lean Management is doubly effective. The Pull system is, on the one hand, a production control system, and, on the other a progress motor. The production control system is the operational implementation and a motor of progress, which, in the end, is more. Plainly, Pull is a progress motor which 'pulls' *Kaizen* .

With the tools of Pull, Lean Management creates a basis for *Kaizen*, visualizes the need for it and distributes the responsibilities and eventually enforces *Kaizen*. The elements of the pull principle are shown below.

5.1 Milk Run

Under the Milk Run principle, Lean Management takes into consideration a round-trip truck that completes daily drives by several suppliers on the same route (Figure 5.1). This means that several suppliers are included in the tour and only the daily consumption of the production is collected. The truck is laterally loaded in the optimum condition.

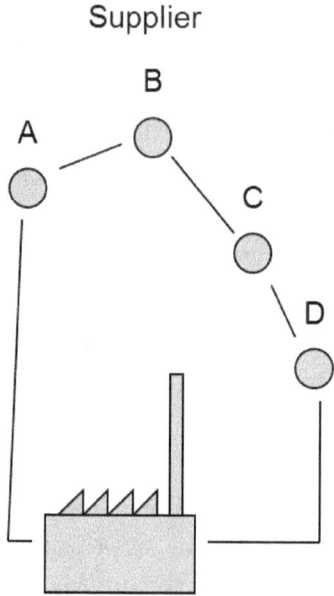

Figure 5.1 Milk run supplier sequence

The milk run allows a daily supply quantity of the production, which depends on the day's demand of the production. This prevents storage of production parts.

5.2 Supermarket

The supermarket is the raw material warehouse in Lean Management. This consists of flow rack, which belong to a fixed assigned part number. The stock has a minimum and maximum quantity, which is displayed visually. The supermarket is supplied directly by the milk run (Figure 5.2).

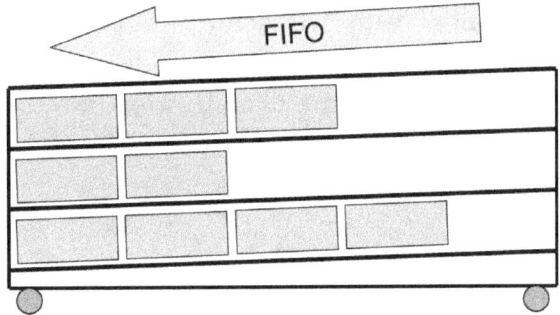

Figure 5.2 Supermarket rack

The supermarket secures FIFO (first in, first out) and represents the bridging between the milk run and the production. In addition, the supermarket visualises the state of the inventory and allows decisions for the procurement of needed goods.

5.3 Small Train

Small Train is a shop floor transport system that runs between the supermarket, WIP (Work in Process), shop stock and TPA (Truck Preparation Area) (Figure 5.3). It is, so to speak, the milk run within the production and ensures the delivery of the different pull tools. This is controlled by a fixed route and multiple *Kanban*.

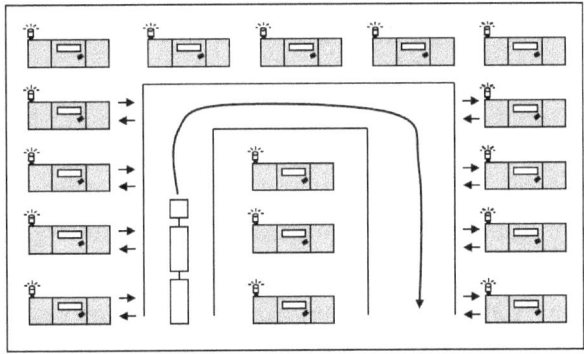

Figure 5.3 A small train route

Thanks to a Small Train, we achieve an efficient supply of production cells and the avoidance of excess stock. In addition, the delivery is standardized and visualisation allows for measures in case of deviation.

5.4 Production cell WIP

The production unit is supplied by the pre-stored raw or not finished material. This is the cell WIP. It is assigned to each cell and is a maximum of twice the consumption volume of the small train cycle. The cell WIP is located directly at the production cell. The cell WIP supplies the production cell until the next cycle. The small train avoids excess inventory and visualizes the material delivery condition.

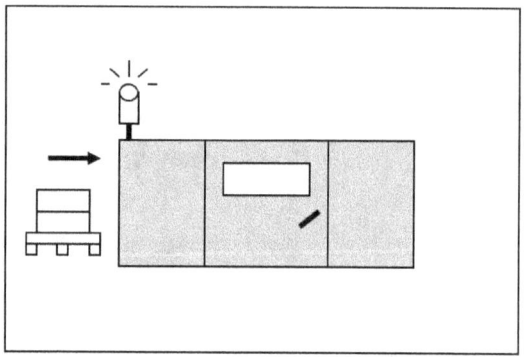

Figure 5.4 Material in front of the machine

5.5 Shop stock

The shop stock represents the storage location of the cell's output. This is located directly on the cell, consists of flow racks and thus ensures FIFO. The shop floor has its own Kanban control loop, which triggers production and defines the quantity within the shop floor (Fig. 5.5).

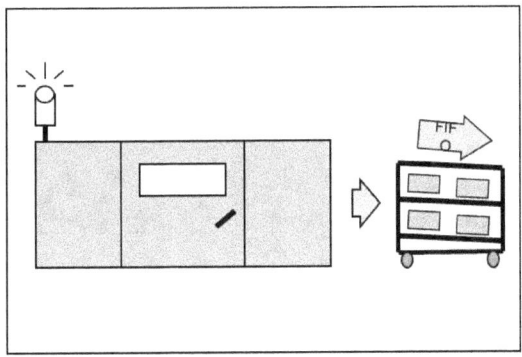

Figure 5.5 Shop stock at the end of a production unit

The shop stock forms the bridging period between the individual production variants. It also visualizes process quality and process reliability by its size and content.

5.6 Kanban

Kanban is the realization of demand-oriented manufacturing (pull principle). The control circuit determines the volume between the source and output. A Kanban card triggers production and accompanies the product until consumption (Figure 5.6).

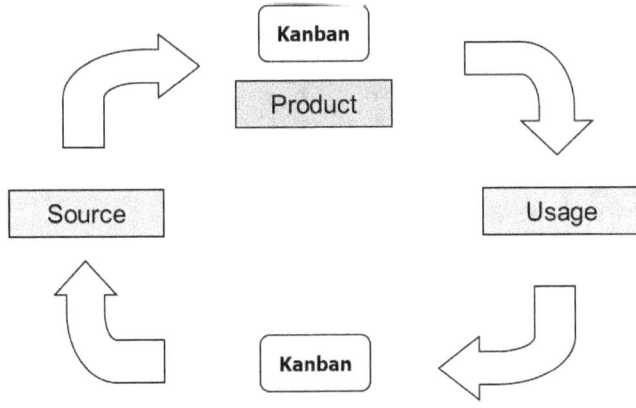

Figure 5.6 Kanban control loop

There are several types of *Kanban*. Here are the three most important ones:

- Production *Kanban* triggers the production start and determine the shop stock
- Small-train *Kanban* gives the signal for the small train to supply the production cell
- *Heijunka Kanban* sets the small train the takt to pick up the finished goods

The kanbans implement the pull idea operationally and visualize the inventory. They are the information carriers for both employees and management.

5.7 Heijunka

The goal of pull production is levelling production. The Heijunka Board is used for this purpose (Fig. 5.7). It sets the takt for the small train, which means the intervals at which the finished products are to be fetched from the shop stock and consequently being delivered to a TPA. This ensures that the production process is levelled and both logistics and production have agreed to the production quantities. The Heijunka Kanban cards provide the signal for this.

Heijunka has the task of reaching an agreement between the various departments; e.g. production and supply chain. It is also intended to balance production and visualize process instability.

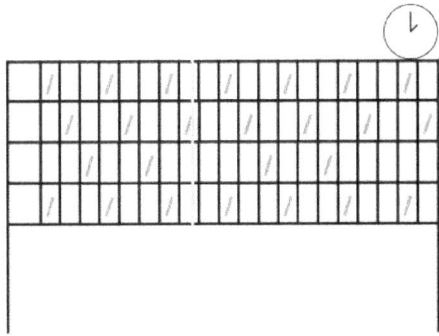

Figure 5.7 Heijunka board

5.8 Truck Preparation Area (TPA)

The last station in the pull system is the Truck Preparation Area (TPA). This forms the delivery dock, in which the pallets are prepared and await delivery to the customer. This is the double nature of a TPA. The TPA is being supplied directly from the shop stock by using the Heijunka Board (Fig. 5.8).

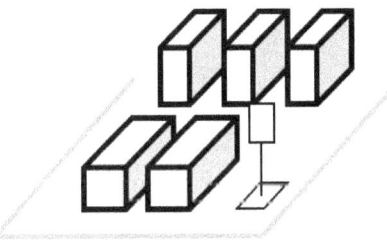

Figure 5.8 Truck Preparation Area

Visualization of the preparation of a customer delivery allows one the ability to react to defective deliveries. It provides a Lean Management routine, forcing management to think and act as a customer.

Based on a Kanban control loop

The automatic moulding machine supplies an assembly line with its work-in-progress. The planning of the moulding unit is carried out by WP/PPC (WP = work preparation, PPC = production planning and control). There are always bottlenecks in certain parts numbers, while others are available in large quantities. Again and again, the assembly staff complains about the unreliable delivery from the moulding department. The supply chain manager, in turn, complains about high inventories. The employees in the automatic moulding department, on the other hand, say that the planning/assembly orders wrong quantities, because they always produce according the production orders.

The management discusses the problems and decides to implement a *Kanban* loop between the assembly line and the moulding shop. For this purpose, the control loop is calculated in the workshop and the shop stock is built up. *Kanbans* are created and attached to the material boxes. All other storage locations are then resolved so that the parts are now stored in front of the machine. Additional measures consist of the formation of the team structure in the moulding shop and SMED workshops (that are carried out). The transport takes place through the Small train.

After half a year the team meets again and looks at the results:
- Inventories are reduced.
- Production takes place according to consumption.
- The defect deliveries are almost eliminated.
- The PPC has been relieved since the machine now controls itself via Kanban.
- Team formation has now been optimized, especially between the two departments.

See Figure 5.5 and Pocket Power "Kanban".

6. TPM

6.1 Basic principles

Total Productive Maintenance (TPM) is a prerequisite for reducing set-up times and increasing machine efficiency. Like all Lean methods and tools, TPM fits into an overall lean concept. This is why TPM does not develop its full effectiveness until further lean methods and instruments are used.

WHAT IS IT ALL ABOUT?

Downtime of machines and plants means waste (*Muda*) and must be eliminated by consistently implementing the Lean idea. Downtimes can have the following causes:

- changeovers
- cycle losses
- poor quality
- unplanned downtime
- planned downtime
- missing material
- micro stops

Total Productive Maintenance is determined by three approaches (Brunner, 2008):

- total machine effectiveness
- total machine maintenance
- total employee participation

Firstly, the machine's effectiveness depends on its visibility (as illustrated by the overall equipment efficiency indicator) and thus provides the decisive indications for starting points for improvement. The term total may, at first glance, appear materialistic. What is meant in this context is the consistent and ruthless elimination of waste. The "pursuit for perfection" is one of the five principles of Lean Management. According to this principle, the plant efficiency is not to be improved a bit, but to be driven to perfection.

Machine maintenance is the subject of maintenance and repair. Here, too, the focus is on procedures and concepts which are aimed at eliminating the failure of systems due to defective parts and for the purpose of preventing system failure due to defective parts and inadequate maintenance. Within the scope of total employee participation, it is to be achieved that the employees, who deal with the means of production in the day-to-day operations, are the first and best starting point for improving the availability of machines. If the employees working on the machine are integrated into the maintenance and repair process, the distance to the production means is reduced and the chances for productivity improvement are increased.

WHY SHOULD WE DO THIS?

If the actual effectiveness of the system remains largely invisible as regards to added value, then installations are not adequately maintained (breakdown maintenance) and repairs may be carried out too late (don't fix it until it is broken). If the potential of the employees is not used to support the machine availability, then the company loses a valuable opportunity to improve technical production resources. No company can afford to do this today.

In 1960, Nippondenso introduced preventive maintenance. At that time, maintenance was carried out by a service department while machine operators merely carried out productive activities. As the automation progressed, more and more personnel were needed in the maintenance department. The company changed the task division so that machine operators were given simple maintenance tasks while the service staff members performed more complex tasks of maintenance and modification of the equipment. The success led to the birth of Total Productive Maintenance. The result was a significantly higher efficiency of the machine and a reduction in the product lifecycle costs for the production machinery.

6.2 Involvement of employees

WHAT IS IT ALL ABOUT?

Real-life situations show that 50% of machine failures are due to insufficient maintenance (e.g., lack of lubrication). The strict separation between the maintenance and production part of machines in most companies leads to a lack of interest and an inadequate responsibility on behalf of the machine operator and becomes a case of not my job-type attitudes.

The employee therefore relies on the service department. The initiative is reduced to calling help from this department in case of problems. However, if the employee is responsible for a faultless function, he or she will identify himself with his machine and have an interest in its well-being.

WHY SHOULD WE DO THIS?

If, however, partial tasks of maintenance are transferred to machine operators, the motivation to keep one's 'own' machine in good operating condition increases. Thus, there is a task division between the maintenance department, which now has capacity for higher-quality tasks, and the employee at the machine, which carries out routine maintenance work.

In a mechanical engineering company, punching machines often failed, even though the service department carried out regular maintenance work. Wearing parts were exchanged preventively, i.e. before their failure.

It turned out that a certain part, which failed prematurely due to a construction error, was responsible for these issues. As a result, further parts of the machine were damaged, so that their replacement became necessary as well. The manufacturer promised an exchange of all affected parts, but a deadline of at least six months was specified, since a complete new design and corresponding tests were necessary.

The employees at the machines indicated on request that increased vibrations occurred before the part failed. Therefore, the relevant employees were involved in the service processes and performed preventive exchanges before a failure could occur. The success of employee involvement was so great that a further expansion of the service tasks was carried out.

6.3 5S method

WHAT IS IT ALL ABOUT?

5S is a very important foundation building block of Lean Management and follows the basic idea of elimination of waste at the level of the individual workplace by standardization of the processes or functions. The standardization determines a once-reached state with a reduced amount of waste and prevents a fall-back in "traditional" behaviours. This creates a basis for the next step towards elimination of still existing waste within the framework of *Kaizen*. Method 5S starts at the workstations of the employees in a process. This may be for example a picking workplace of a warehouse employee. Though there are regulations for safety at work in most countries, this alone does not guarantee the efficiency of the work to be carried out.

It is also important to consider the fact that employees have to change between different jobs and then have to deal with a new environment. The more homogeneous and well-arranged the workplaces are organized, the quicker an employee can work efficiently in his/her new workplace.

5S denotes the following Japanese terms:

- *Seiri* (sort): Necessary and unnecessary items are being separated, tools and materials that are no longer needed are being removed. This keeps the workplace neat.
- *Seiton* (set): Everything that is needed for the work is to be kept in such a way that it is ready for use. Cabinets and shelves are marked with the items to be kept there, eliminating the need to search for materials or tools.
- *Seiso* (shine): A workplace that is clean, relieves the detection of errors and increases the quality of the work. Contamination of materials is avoided; the workplace is tidy and well-arranged.
- *Seiketsu* (standardize): Guidelines and instructions for the execution of tasks lead to the elimination of doubts about the activities. Work instructions and workflows have to become routine and visible at the workplace (example: Mc Donald's).
- *Shitsuke* (sustain): Employees should be motivated to comply with specifications and work instructions. In addition, a continuous improvement process is to be initiated. The employees' suggestions for improvement should be honoured and the improved performance of the employees should be made visible to all.

WHY SHOULD WE DO THIS?

Due to improved clarity and order, the processing times at individual workstations are reduced (tools are found without searching, material is immediately accessible, no unnecessary objects are in the way and impede the process). This results in cost reductions. Material is more readily available and the amount required is reduced. Often material is present in a workplace environment, but it is so unkempt that it is not found. Therefore, replenishment is more often carried out from the warehouse than is necessary.

Standards for the design of procedures and the execution of tasks facilitate the takeover by new employees and help to avoid errors.

In the context of a *Kaizen* project "Elimination of waste in the office" in a large insurance company, the following forms of waste were determined during the observation of a desk workplace:
- Often many minutes passed until a process was found in the folders of the PC.
- The path to the files in which the completed transactions were filed was relatively long.
- Numerous unprocessed operations covered the surfaces.
- The cursor in the screen of the database program often had to be moved over longer distances.
- In the event of queries and the obtaining of decisions and signatures from the supervisor, unproductive waiting times were incurred.
- The operating system was partly not available or IT support was required.

With 5S the workplace was reorganized. Afterwards, the procedures and tasks were standardized. Subsequently, the processes were improved. The self-steering of the employees and the strengthening of self-responsibility have eliminated a significant portion of waste.

6.4 Equipment effectiveness and equipment maintenance

WHAT IS IT ALL ABOUT?

A consistent implementation of the flow principle means high availability of the production facilities. A material flow in the production process, which is interrupted by failure of machines, makes any Lean concept fail in its approach. This makes TPM an indispensable "mosaic stone" in Lean Management.

The flow principle without interruption is achieved in the concept of Total Productive Maintenance not only by the involvement of employees who operate the equipment and machines, but also by specifically designed maintenance.

WHY SHOULD WE DO THIS?

Due to the TPM concept, the break-down maintenance, which was still practiced in the 1950s, was replaced by a maintenance oriented to 100% availability. Consequently, this principle of total plant maintenance starts already from the point of purchasing equipment and machines.

A procurement directed at TPM is geared to the following requirements (see Brunner 2008):

- Preparation of a technical specification before starting the procurement activities.
- The operating personnel and maintenance department have to take into account the information available in the plant about existing installations.
- Use the identified problems and deficiencies of existing plants for specifications of a new plant.
- Incorporate innovative characteristics of new systems in terms of efficiency and safety.

- Consideration of the maintenance during specification phase (accessibility, if necessary maintenance-free, duration of the standstills for maintenance).
- Integration of training concepts into procurement.
- Acceptance of the system exclusively at 100% fulfilment of the specification.

After the purchase of a machine, further measures are necessary to maintain the machine availability at a high level. One component is a defined maintenance program. In this principle, process orientation and flow are in the spotlights. Changes in the characteristics and performance of the system during operation must be recognized quickly. Regular inspections and a shift to the desired condition are given to the plant's performance.

Preventive maintenance is another component of total plant maintenance. System components which are subject to wear must be replaced before failure if the flow is not to be interrupted unplanned. Depending on the technical concept of the system, either replacement of wear parts according to corresponding time schedules is provided, or the degree of wear is detected by sensors and an exchange takes place when a defined state is reached which necessitates an exchange.

Heidelberger Druckmaschinen produces printing presses at a world-class level. With a remote service, the company offers its customers a unique service, which prevents unexpected production downtime and thus considerable problems for the printing companies.

The Xenon light, which is essential for the operation of a printing machine, is subject to wear but its lifespan cannot be precisely determined. A control device on the machine detects the light intensity of the lamp. This indicates the necessity for an exchange. This in turn triggers an alarm at Heidelberger Druckmaschinen, which is transmitted via the Internet.

There, an exchange of the lamp is being initiated, which can thus be carried out before the critical failure of the lamp.

In addition, Heidelberger Druckmaschinen offers a proactive remote service for the machines manufactured by the company. If one of the machines used in printing plants has a technical problem, the manufacturer is informed by a so-called eCall. An expert from Heidelberger Druckmaschinen will be informed and will get in touch with the printing company. If the customer desires support for the problem, an automated data pre-analysis is carried out, so that an expert from the manufacturer can provide the employees of the printing company with qualified information for solving the problem. In addition, an expert can access the electronic control system of the printing press and directly correct any faults.

The benefits to the printing companies are obvious: in most cases (about 70%) electronic problems with the printing machines can be solved by remote access. There is no need to wait for a service engineer from the manufacturer, thus, the machine down times are drastically reduced. Follow-up costs due to delayed delivery of the products of the printing presses are also significantly reduced. This results in a higher availability of the machines and a timely delivery of the printed products.

7. SMED - Single Minute Exchange of Die

7.1 Basic principles

WHAT IS IT ALL ABOUT?

Single Minute Exchange of The (SMED) is considered a success story in manufacturing facility management. The shortening of machine changeover times and, consequently, the throughput times in production could be achieved by this method to an almost unbelievable extent. However, no concept was misunderstood so often and many operations managers were disappointed with the results after the implementation of the SMED idea in their company. Where does this reproach come from?

First of all, it is to be noted that while the reduction in throughput times in general, it is the changeover times of machines in particular that are a major factor in production management of almost all companies. This is as a result of the perception that production speed is a value or goal per se.

In Lean Management, the following causal chain is put into the foreground: The pull principle requires an adjustment of the production speed or lead time to the requirements of its customer. In almost all sectors, a customer also requires production variants, some of which require equipment retooling. According to Lean-understanding, however, large batch sizes and thus inventories are waste (Muda). The reduction of the changeover time is therefore used to reduce the lot size and thus the inventories (of semi-finished products).

However, if one reduces the set-up times exclusively to increase the output quantity of plants, the availability increases, but also the inventory level and therefore the waste. This shows very clearly the necessity of embedding SMED into a Lean overall concept and the interdependence of all methods and tools.

WHY SHOULD WE DO THIS?

Set-up time reduction is therefore not an objective on its own, so it must be embedded in an overall design concept of the production process in the sense of "value stream without interruption". If a set-up time reduction is used to produce different variants more often and to smooth the value stream, the total throughput time will be reduced without taking "point accelerations" (use of fast machines to reduce the total throughput time).

7.2 Reduction of set-up times

The reduction in set-up times and the application of the SMED methodology in practice can be carried out in four stages. The starting point is a sequential processing of the work required for the conversion (status quo). The conversion time is reduced in four stages:

- Shifting pre-processing and follow-up activities: In the first step, upstream and downstream tasks, such as preparing necessary tools and materials as well as the clean-up after the conversion, are carried out during the ongoing production.
- Separation of internal and external set-up steps: The changeover process itself is subdivided into an internal component (retooling while the machine or system is at a standstill) and an external component (retooling while the machine or plant is still running). This is achieved by means of checklists, optimization of tool transports, and carrying out functional tests during the operational machine time.

- Conversion from internal to external changeover: this can further reduce the downtime of the system or machine. Measures to achieve this goal are, for instance, standardization of tasks, tools and necessary parts; use of intermediate clamping devices, which facilitate the assembly of tools and moulds; pre-assembly of components for the changeover tool and so on.
- Reduction of the time required for internal changeover: the changeover times required during a standstill of the system can be further shortened by performing parallel operations. This can be achieved by means of quick-release fasteners for fastening moulds and modules, as well as by avoiding adjustment work by changing the technical design.

In many cases, a reduction of the changeover time to 5% of the initial value can be achieved by realizing the above described method.

The reduction of changeover times by SMED comprises four steps:

1. Relocation, preparation and post-treatment
2. Separation of internal and external changeover
3. Conversion internal to external changeover
4. Reduction of internal changeover

Figure 7.1 shows the effect of SMED in an overview. The production of parts 1 and 2 occur parallel.

SMED - Single Minute Exchange of Die

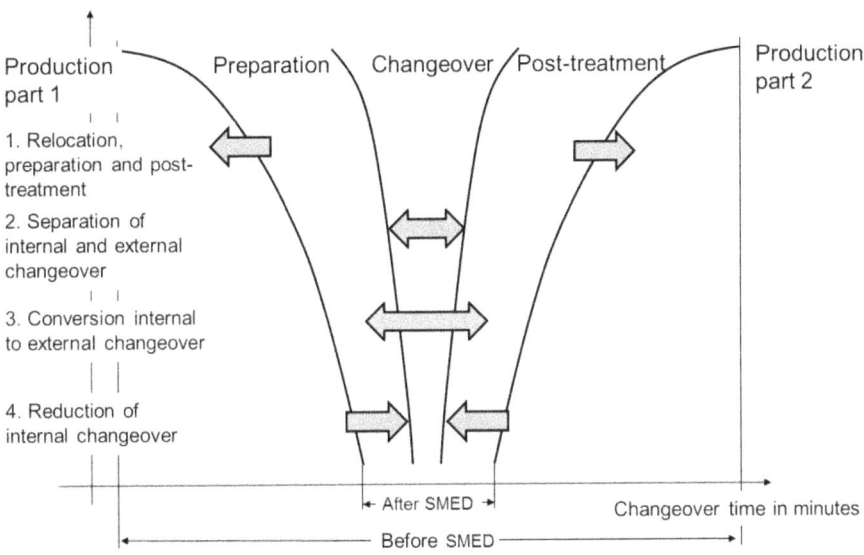

Figure 7.1 Reduction of changeover times through SMED

8. Error proofing

8.1 Poka Yoke

WHAT IS IT ALL ABOUT?

Shigeo Shingo's zero-defect production is based on the following steps:

- Cause analysis,
- 100% control,
- immediate corrections.

Poka Yoke is the fault prevention technique from Lean Management. Its goal is to avoid errors that can be caused by humans. The reason for this is the assumption that every process, which is determined by a human being, has a high potential for errors. In *Poka Yoke*, possible sources of errors are identified and systematically solved by solution approaches, e.g. technical nature can be neutralized. So:

- Discover -> make sure that the error is discovered.
- Avoid -> make the mistake impossible.

Product Poka Yoke

Product Poka Yoke is mainly error prevention during usage. Here, the design or description prevents the user from causing errors (Figure 8.1).

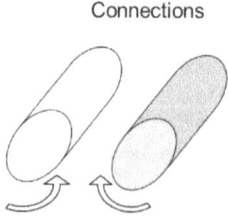

Figure 8.1 Prevention of mixing up connectors

Process Poka Yoke

Process Poka Yoke aims at avoiding errors during the manufacturing process and increases the required quality (Fig. 8.2). As such, the Poka Yoke process is focused on both product development and manufacturing.

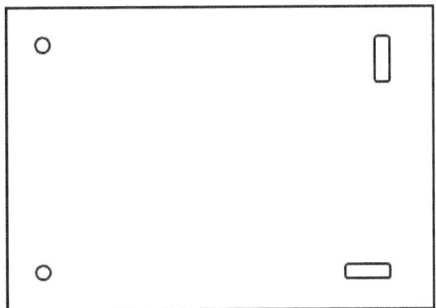

Figure 8.2 Error free assembly

Hard and soft Poka Yoke

During the implementation of Poka Yoke, a distinction is made between hard and soft Poka Yoke.

Hard Poka Yoke
Faults are avoided by constructive measures. These allow the employee to cause a fault only by major negligence.

Soft Poka Yoke
Soft Poka Yoke is to be understood as a measure which indicates to the employee a possible source of error and which is trying to be avoided. For example, cross-scanning (by either personnel or computer systems).

It is important that the corrective measures are immediately initialized. These might be of a soft *Poka Yoke* nature, followed by the hard ones. Hereby, there are both primary and secondary sources of errors.

Poka Yoke is a key factor in the qualitative success of Lean companies by ensuring that a mistake is made impossible. *Poka Yoke* is not exclusively used for manufacturing, but is being used in every process step along the way.

WHY SHOULD WE DO THIS?

Poka Yoke is a tool of Lean Management to implement a zero-defect strategy and promotes the high quality of *Kaizen*. Quality is not just about product quality but also quality of the process. This results in higher customer satisfaction and cost savings as well as releases resources which, in turn, are used to generate Kaizen or to achieve additional sales.

Poka Yoke Office

One example of a zero-defect culture in a company outside of manufacturing is the handing over of work sequences. If an employee sends documents to the next step in the process, then they will only be accepted if they are error-free and complete. The documents are created in such a way that only numbers can be entered in those fields where numbers are required.

8.2 Failure Mode and Effects Analysis (FMEA)

WHAT IS IT ALL ABOUT?

Products and services which are faulty designed, developed, produced or created, and which are sent defective to the customer, lead to additional costs for the responsible company. For:

- rework
- loss of value due to disposal/scrap

- transport costs for return and replacement
- sales decline due to loss of image and trust among customers
- replacements for consequential damages

These costs are all the greater the later the errors are discovered in the supply chain (Fig. 8.3).

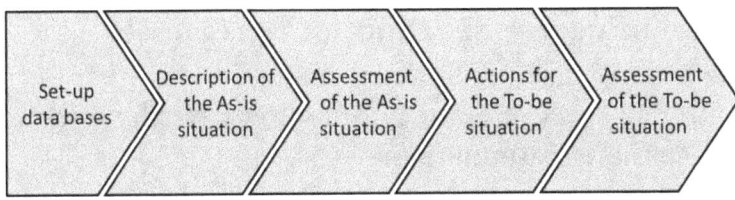

Figure 8.3 Process steps of FMEA

In Lean Management, these costs are waste (Muda). A product that is faulty can, for example, result in a loss of value and additional costs.

WHY SHOULD WE DO THIS?

An effective tool within the framework of Lean Management is Failure Mode and Effects Analysis (FMEA). Failure Mode and Effects Analysis is a formalized method to systematically and completely capture possible problems, their risks and consequences even before they emerge. Figure 8.3 shows the individual steps of FMEA.

Early detection of errors pays off. With every step along the value chain, the value of the product or the service will be added to the cost value. If this value is added to an already faulty product, the effort is wasted. The customer will not be willing to pay the purchase price for this, or he will claim a reduction.

In the worst-case scenario, the defective product must be disposed of or recycled at a high cost, and the customer must be supplied with a fault-free product at short notice. Apart from the negative effect on the reputation of the supplying company, additional costs have incurred, all of which reduces the company's overall success.

In the following, the process steps within an FMEA are presented in an example (commissioning in a distribution warehouse).

Commissioning in a distribution warehouse

Data collection
In this first step, all relevant information describing the process under discussion is summarized:
- Definition of the commissioning process
- Collection of suppliers and procurement processes of the goods for commissioning
- Recipients/customers of consignments

Description of the As-Is state
How is the process carried out today? What are possible problems?
- Picking of goods for shipment to customers
- Picking error (goods missing, goods not ordered, wrong address)
- Causes (Error in incoming order, faulty picking, theft)

Evaluation of the As-Is state
How serious are the errors? How often do these occur, which problems are to be addressed first?
- Probability of errors
- Significance of the errors for the customer
- Cost of errors for the company
- Probability of discovery before delivery to the customer
- Determination of the priority figure

Measures for the To-Be state
How could we avoid these errors in the future? What measures should be implemented first?
- Development of measures with high risk priority
- New systems of picking, such as pick-by-voice, radio frequency identification systems
- recording of orders with control loops

Evaluation of the To-Be state
How did the error rate change after implementation of the measures? Did we achieve our goals? Where can further improvements be achieved?
- Collection of picking errors and reconciliation with the target/To-Be value
- Calculation of a new risk priority number
- Decision for further improvement measures

8.3 Total Quality Management

WHAT IS IT ALL ABOUT?

Total Quality Management is a "... management approach of an organisation centred on quality, based on the participation of all its members and aiming at long term success through customer satisfaction and benefits to all members of the organisation and society.... " (formerly from ISO 8402).

As mentioned, one of the pillars of Lean Management is the Pull principle. Together with visualization, these two important elements of Lean Management are combined in Total Quality Management. Visualization in TQM means the visualization of customer needs throughout the entire process chain of creating a product or service.

In many companies the relationship to the customer and his needs are lost during the course of the service creation process. The employees focus merely on the respective tasks and activities they consider necessary. The product developer realizes, for example, his idea of quality of the product, but forgets that quality is exclusively defined by the customer. This is part of the service agreement between a customer and its supplier or manufacturer.

If, on the other hand, the customer requirements or, better, the quality requirements of the customer are transparently communicated throughout the service creation process, then these become visible to everyone involved in the process and the chances of achieving customer satisfaction are clearly improved. Customer orientation is therefore one of the pillars of TQM.

WHY SHOULD WE DO THIS?

The pull principle means that all activities in a supply chain have the customer as starting point. By consistently aligning companies over the entire supply chain to the customer needs, waste is avoided (only what the customer wants) and customer satisfaction is achieved (the customer receives the quality he expects).

The most important components of TQM are:

- Customer orientation (orientation of quality to customer requirements)
- Process orientation (Process design according to accepted principles of process management, cf. Füermann and Dammasch 2008)
- Involvement of employees (employee orientation)
- Avoiding waste (elimination of non-value-added activities)
- Use of statistical tools for process control

In a consultancy firm, a customer survey was conducted in respect to meeting customer satisfaction of a consulting project. Customer satisfaction was one of the elements of the so-called "quality management manual", in which the quality objectives and processes of the company were documented.

In this customer satisfaction analysis, around 60% of the surveyed customers showed that the "friendliness of the telephone service" was rated as particularly high, whereas "compliance with deadlines" was rated as rather unsatisfactory by the same respondents.

The survey was carried out taking into account a two-dimensional approach. In other words, the importance of each criterion was questioned. Further important conclusions can be drawn from this.

Most customers only attached few importance to "friendliness of the telephone service". This means that the customer is "pampered" and thus receives a service which obviously is of little value to him. Money is wasted here (and possibly also customer time).

The criterion of "compliance with final deadlines", on the other hand, was highly valued by customers. Therefore one sees that there was an urgent need for action. The consultancy company has immediately introduced a new method for controlling project progress in order to solve the problem of customer dissatisfaction as soon as possible.

9. Sustainable and continuous Kaizen

WHAT IS IT ALL ABOUT?

The success of a project depends on its organization and the method of activity action and actors in the project. These should be guided into the right path for the process. PDCA is a problem-solving process consisting of four phases. The background to this classification is the assumption that a successful improvement process always requires certain sequences and steps. PDCA is based on a hypothesis methodology, i.e. a scientifically based assumption, which must be proved or rejected. This is achieved by statistical process monitoring. Another aspect is that a stabilization of the process can only take place if extensive process knowledge exists and if this knowledge is applied.

WHY SHOULD WE DO THIS?

The four phases of PDCA (Figure 9.1) are pictured as a cycle and lead to a recurring cycle that starts with the Plan phase but does not end, as mistakenly assumed, with the Act phase. Instead, the cycle returns to "Plan" after execution of the Act phase. This mechanism automatically starts the next improvement. The PDCA methodically guides the employees through actions/projects and forces them to follow each phase meticulously. This results in sustainable implementation, which results from solving the true problem and its symptoms. This is the PDCA's doctrine.

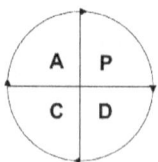

Figure 9.1 PDCA cycle (Plan – Do – Check – Act)

It should be noted that the PDCA cycle should not only be used on workshop level but rather at all levels of within a company.

9.1 Plan

Under the Plan phase (Fig. 9.2), we do not only understand the chronological planning, but more the analysis of the problem. Following steps are executed:

- Definition of problem and objectives.
- Actual and target values are compared with each other and the deviation is determined.
- Determine the method to analyse the problem.
- Analysis to understand the problem with Lean tools.
- Detailed analysis of the problem and the data as well as the definition of the problem causes.
- Definition of the presumed approaches with the aim of finding sustainable, fast and cheap solutions.

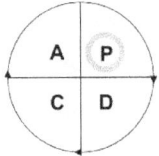

Figure 9.2 Plan phase

9.2 Do

The Plan phase has now been completed. The Do phase (Figure 9.3) is different depending on the complexity of the project. Generally speaking, the solution approaches in the plan phase are to be converted into hypotheses. Then the hypotheses are tested (Do). Two possible scenarios are to be depicted:

- For simple projects, the solution approach is implemented and tested immediately after the description of the

hypothesis. Thus, the Do phase represents the transformation phase.
- For more complex projects, the test phase is carried out after the hypothesis has been set up. Thereafter we try to prove the thesis. The reaction is thus carried out after the test. The Do phase reflects the pure test phase.

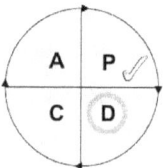

Figure 9.3 Do phase

9.3 Check

During the Check phase (Figure 9.4) the implementations (simple projects) or the hypothesis test (more complex projects) are evaluated. The expectations generated in the plan phase are compared with the results from the Do phase. Here comes the following result:

- Has the implementation (hypothesis) reached its expectation or not?
- The hypothesis is now confirmed or rejected.

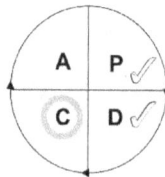

Figure 9.4 Check phase

This results in a widening of knowledge, since confirming or rejecting the hypotheses now classifies the individual factors as effective or ineffective.

9.4 Act/Standard

The Act phase (Figure 9.5) is the reaction to the results of the Plan and Check phase. Decisions are made based on the results of the investigations and targets. It is determined whether or not the improvement has reached its goal and can be 'finished' or not.

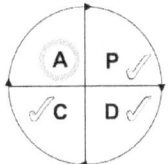

Figure 9.5 Act phase

- Improvement/project completion now leads to the decision to start a new plan phase, that is, to tackle another problem. The completion of the improvement is not the successful investigation, but the implementation of acquired knowledge. So new standards have to be implemented with a conversion plan, which will then be translated into a living standard.
- The non-fulfilment of the objectives leads to a correction, i.e. the return to the original plan phase. The gained knowledge has been processed and a new plan is created. This phase runs in compliance with the PDCA cycle. This is done until the target is reached.

With PDCA the improvement and workshop participants are forced into a system during a project. In addition, the results must be checked for efficacy. Only in case of lasting success, completion of a project will be ensured. In addition, PDCA forces the next improvement. This results in permanent Kaizen.

9.5 PDCA and Hoshin Kanri

WHAT IS IT ALL ABOUT?

It is worth mentioning that the PDCA Cycle or an improvement does not refer exclusively to improvements in production units or workshop improvement, but that it takes place at all levels of a company and includes the management as well. Unfortunately, this is disregarded in many Lean Management implementations.

The PDCA Cycle is seen as a method of change in lean companies, both on horizontal and vertical levels. As a result, the PDCA group is also used to implement *Hoshin Kanri*/Policy Deployment. For each level, a PDCA is created, which in turn generates multiple PDCAs.

WHY SHOULD WE DO THIS?

The goal is to cascade and systematically process the company's objectives. PDCA allows us to ask the right questions at our management level and to take the right measures. If these are not as effective as they were planned, the PDCA forces corrective measures (Fig. 9.6).

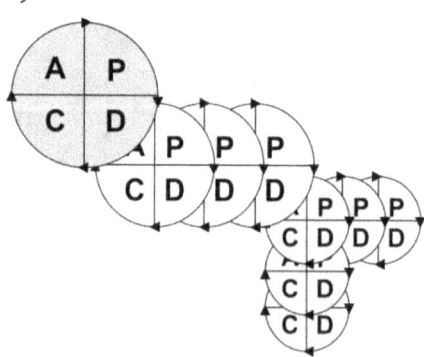

Figure 9.6 Check phase

9.6 A3 report/A3 paper

WHAT IS IT ALL ABOUT?

The methodical approach of A3 reporting (also known as A3 paper) is analogous to that of a PDCA Cycle, whereby the A3 report can also be divided into seven steps. The A3 report is used for more complex problems and challenges. In doing so, the document is used by management and specialists to initiate an improvement and present a project.

The name "A3" refers to the format of the report because it is limited to a DIN A3 page. An A3 report changes during a project or team improvement. This means that through the systematic approach, which includes the analysis phase, the document gains maturity. This development of knowledge and team improvements is reflected in different versions of the document.

WHY SHOULD WE DO THIS?

The A3 report is divided into systematic questions, so that a systematic and methodical processing of the questionnaire/process is followed. The restriction to an A3 format places great emphasis on visualisation. The creator must be able to present the entire question or problem situation, as well as the progress of the solution path and the current project status, in the shortest possible time. Thus, A3 reporting asks for systematics and methodology just like the PDCA Cycle does. This in combination with a compulsion to concentrate on the essential and the visual (Figure 9.7).

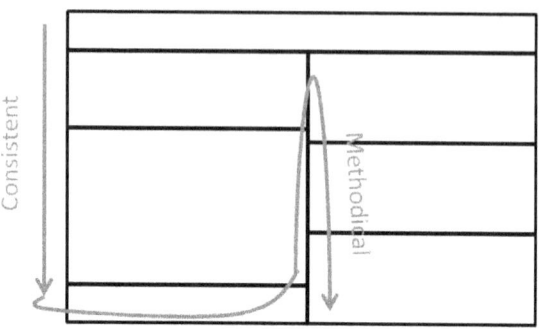

Figure 9.7 A3 report

9.7 8D report

8D reporting (Fig. 9.8) supports a systematic approach to major problems or cases where the cause is not immediately apparent. In contrast to PDCA, the methodical steps in an 8D report are not abstract or divided into several steps. For example, To the "P" (plan) phase involves several steps: Problem description, analysis, numbers/data/facts, target deviation, problem solving hypotheses (ideas) and hypothesis plan.

In an 8D report, the methodological approach is already much clearer and allows for easier processing. This is why 8D reporting finds such a high application in (amongst many others) complaints handling.

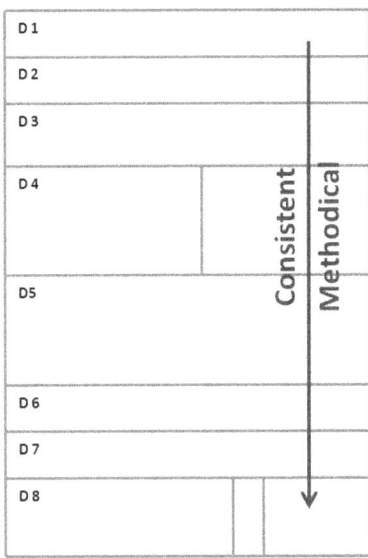

Figure 9.8 8D report

The "D" refers to disciplines or stages in which the report is created. The following steps are used to create the report: formation of a team, description of the problem/defect character, immediate measures (containment or quarantine), investigation of its error causes, selection of problem solutions, implementation of problem solving solutions, preventing repetition of errors and assessment of the success of the team. The 8D report has the same steps as PDCA and the A3 report. The main difference is that the 8D report places great emphasis on containment (quarantine) in order to avoid further spreading of the problem. This is why 8D reporting is particularly suitable for customer complaints (external and internal) and for work accidents.

The 8D report is an example of a methodology frequently used in the automotive industry, which has been standardized in a form by the "Verband der Automobilindustrie" (VDA, Association of the Automotive Industry).

10. Lean Development

Under Lean Development (LD), Lean Management understands the development of new products and processes under the aspects of Lean Management, such as flow, production, supply chain, etc. Additionally, it refers to the incorporation of experiences gained from *Kaizen* activities such as *Kaizen* workshops. New developments are being tested and examined for their manufacturing complexity. This means that the products need to be both customer and production specific oriented. Another aspect of Lean Management is the design of a development process according to the aspects of Lean Management, such as one-piece flow processes or zero-defect processes.

10.1 U-cells and Chaku Chaku cells

U-cell

WHAT IS IT ALL ABOUT?

The term U-cell refers to the U-shaped design of a production unit. This production unit is designed according to the one-piece flow principle. In other words, there are no manufacturing buffers between workstations. Moreover, this U-cell can be operated by one or more persons. This means that production can react flexibly to customer requirements. In doing so, one avoids waste (Muda), in particular avoidance of transport, is of great importance.

WHY SHOULD WE DO THIS?

The main advantage of this production unit is the possibility to balance a production after customer interaction and thus the avoidance of inventory. In addition, a fixed number of employees does not have to be used, but can be adapted to the customer's requirements. Each cell is designed so that there are no material buffers between stations. As a result, the entire production cell comes to a standstill as soon as one station causes an error. This situation combined with manufacturing according to the customer's tact, forces a company to rectify errors immediately in order to avoid compromising product delivery to the customer.

The company Schmid manufactures manually assembled electrical connectors. Each individual process step has high stocks (20 days lead time) and is not connected to the next one. For some time, Lean Management has been introduced and the team has decided to convert the manufacturing to the U-cell (Figure 10.1).

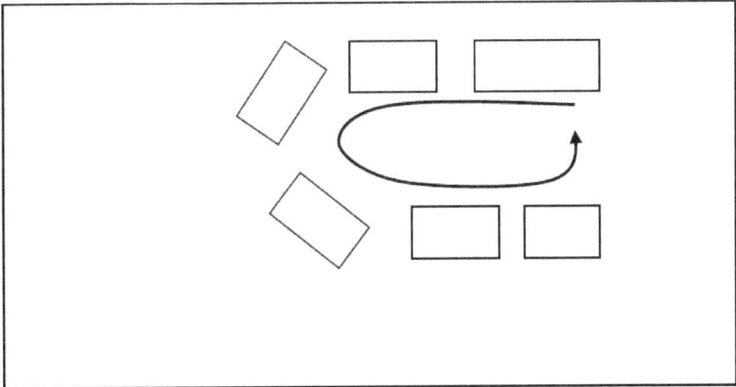

Figure 10.1 U-cell

The individual workstations are built up in a U according to their sequence. Only one set (one piece flow) is taken into account so that the individual stations can be reduced in size. This change in layout has resulted in a space saving. The individual process steps of the employees are now balanced and standardized according to the volume. A team structure is introduced.

The result of the project is a reduction of the lead time to one day and a flexible occupation of each U-cell with up to four employees. By reducing non-value-added activities, profitability increases at the same time. The team is now starting to plan other *Kaizen* campaigns, as weaknesses and potentials have been revealed through applying this one-piece flow philosophy.

Chaku Chaku cell

WHAT IS IT ALL ABOUT?

The *Chaku-Chaku* cell is the advanced version of a U-cell. Workstations are manually loaded and automatically unloaded. The individual work steps in the stations are now no longer carried out by employees but are automated. In this case, the employee only loads one station after another.

WHY SHOULD WE DO THIS?

The goal here is to increase the degree of automation while minimizing the costs of personnel, investment and operations. There is also a possibility to avoid complicated, automated loading processes and avoiding automating the unloading process as well. The human skills are concentrated on the complex processes and the controllable, simpler processes are being automated. Lean Management, as it applies *Chaku-Chaku*, achieves a higher availability of production units while reducing personnel, investments and operating costs.

In the company's annual plan it was noted that product A must be further rationalized due to severe competition. Since five employees are working on this U-cell, the major part of costs can be assigned to salary payments. The management decides to convert the U-cell into a Chaku-Chaku cell.

The existing stations are being rebuilt with a supplier, so employees only have to load them. This means that some stations have now been automated. Unloading is automatic. Today, the employee loads station one and removes the already processed and ejected part from this station. Now, he goes immediately to station two. He does not wait during processing.

The same principle applies here: loading and at the same time taking out the produced part. The structure of the cell corresponds to the U-cell philosophy and has hardly changed. This cell can now be operated with only one or two employees.

This means that the conversion reduces the number of operators on the one hand, while, at the same time, increasing productivity. On the other hand, the high investment costs are avoided for a fully automated operation.

10.2 Cardboard workshop and Minimum Technical Solution

Cardboard Workshop

WHAT IS IT ALL ABOUT?

A machine or production cell is replicated and simulated by using carton boxes during a workshop. Various participants from the company participate in this method of re-enacting the process and carefully research the new equipment for value-adding and non-value-adding process steps as well as for the actual applicability of the machine design in the production process.

WHY SHOULD WE DO THIS?

The integration of errors and the knowledge gained from Kaizen activities and workshops flow into the new layout. The implemented improvements are, together with employees and suppliers, integrated into a simulation, this means, ideas are tested directly on the cardboard model.

Minimum Technical Solution

WHAT IS IT ALL ABOUT?

The technical requirements are aligned to the minimum technical requirements to reduce overall investment. It also ensures that lean management principles, such as One-Piece Flow or SMED, are adhered to. The production staff assesses the simulated process according to their experiences and problems and elaborate improvements. The know-how collected in the database is reconciled. The resulting further development is now integrated into the overall process and examined according to supply chain aspects as well as to corresponding utilization of the overall concept. A cardboard workshop is launched and the Minimum Technical Solutions are examined. This is a process value stream analysis which concentrates on production machines.

WHY SHOULD WE DO THIS?

Applying this concept, Lean Management intends to reduce the amount to be invested and to avoid excessive, non-value adding technology. In addition, the entire concept is revised and implemented according to the lean philosophy.

Cardboard workshop and Minimum Technical Solution

Many months of dedication of the sales staff was rewarded by winning a contract. This contract entailed both big opportunities and risks for the medium-sized car supplier. On the one hand, the success of the new model could have been attributed to high unit numbers and sales. On the other hand, the high investment in a fully automated machine had a high capital commitment. In case of small numbers of units in the start-up phase or a moderate success of the model, the car supplier will be confronted with high fixed costs and entrepreneurial risks.

Moreover, it will be confronted with the challenge of technical controllability.

The spokesman responsible for the division decides to revise the solution developed by Manufacturing Engineering (full automatic machine) in a workshop. The team includes both responsible engineers and employees from production, quality, maintenance, purchasing and logistics. The team starts with reproducing the machine with cardboards. The principles of Cardboard Workshop and Minimum Technical Solution are applied. The employees test the applicability with the model by stimulating manufacturing. They are investigating the concept for value-enhancing processes and simulating the degree of automation combined with the experience of shop floor workers. The results, as always, are presented to the management, and the decision is made.

The workshop has led to the following improvements:
- Introduction of parts automation as a first step
- Adapting the concept to the needs of production
- Removal of conveyor belts, automatic loading and buffer systems
- Implementation of First Defect Stop
- One Piece Flow alignment and size reduction of the machine
- Facilitating maintenance work
- New specification document, which was developed in the second workshop with the suppliers
- Reduction of required machine investments

11. Six Sigma

Another method that has established itself alongside Lean Management is Six Sigma. The emphasis has been placed on quality assurance, which is to be achieved using statistical tools and accurate data analyses of the actual process. Relevant process data, such as process characteristics, errors and parameters, are collected and statistically evaluated. The team structure in Six Sigma consists of Sponsor, Champion, Black Belt and Green Belt. In contrast to Lean Management, Six Sigma is a project that marks the beginning of an experiment for improvement.

The term sigma (σ) defines the parameter for the process capability. Six Sigma therefore means six times the standard deviation, whereby the sigma values are set in relation to the measured quantity ppm (parts per million). The goal is to reach 6 σ, i.e. 3.4 ppm.

Six Sigma relies on a process of improvement and team building, which takes place in five phases, the so-called DMAIC cycles. The cycle includes the Define, Measure, Analyse, Improve, and Control phases:

Define

>The Define phase is the creation phase of the project contract. This is where the tasks and objectives for the teams are worked out and defined.

Measure

>The hypotheses are defined. Subsequently, the associated measuring methods are defined and data are collected. For this purpose, the feasibility of data collection must be clarified in advance.

Analyse

> After Measure, analysis is the next step. Here the measurements are identified, verified and quantified according to causes. Attempts are made to conclude from the measurements on the cause of error and to provide evidence of the validity of the identified cause.

Improve

> During the improvement phase, an attempt is made to find a solution to the problem that is both cost-saving and effective. The measurement values are defined in order to quantify the financial effect of the improvement. In addition, a risk analysis and a conversion plan are generated. This is followed by the implementation itself.

Control

> Here, the improvement is examined based on its sustainability, the actual measurement variables are compared to the plan measurement variables and deviations are recorded and documented. Upon completion, the integration of the changed process into a process standard is carried out. If necessary, new projects are defined.

12. Tools of Lean Management

12.1 Seven statistical tools

The seven statistical tools are also referred to in the literature as "seven quality tools" ("Q7") (see Kamiske/Brauer 2008b). The use of these tools in the corporate environment is possible without extensive training of employees and should help to identify and solve problems in a company. The tools are predominantly visually oriented. This is why the application is associated with the advantage of being immediately eye-catching.

Error list

The error list (Fig. 12.1) is used to easily record errors of operational activities. Errors such as semi-finished products arrive at a machine which are to be processed further, or interruptions of assembly processes as a result of missing material, are noted.

Parts not within tolerances	|||
Too little parts in container	ﾊｲ
Arrival material train too late	ﾊｲ ﾊｲ
Wrong parts	|||
Delivery of parts only on request	ﾊｲ ﾊｲ |||

Figure 12.1 Error list

The first step before creating the list is categorizing the error types. On the one hand, this is to be done pragmatically so that the amount of error types is not excessive, on the other hand, no important categories may be missing. Too many types of errors in the list make entry more difficult. If there are too few types of error, the category "other errors" may have too many elements, resulting in a poorly usable error list.

After evaluating the results, the errors with the highest frequency and the greatest expected error costs can be filtered out and eliminated in the context of an improvement project.

Histogram

The histogram, or column graph, is an instrument to show the frequency distribution of data ordered by class. For this purpose, for example, measured values are recorded over the diameter of a lathing part. Classes are formed, that is, intervals are defined in which the measured value is assigned to a class. The result is a distribution of measured values, see figure 12.2.

From these values we can deduce which lie within a required or predetermined tolerance. The measured values outside this tolerance are then the starting point of projects to reduce these undesirable deviations from the target corridor.

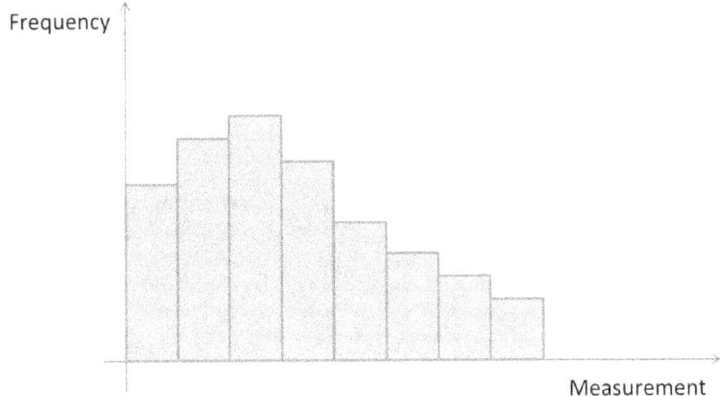

Figure 12.2 Histogram

Quality control card

The control card is used to monitor manufacturing processes. It aims to detect any undesirable development of the measured values in order to counteract them on time.

The prerequisite for using the quality control card is a controlled process. This means that measured values are only randomly scattered over the result of the process (e.g., a lathing part). This can be further explained by Figure 12.3.

Firstly, an average value (target value) and the deviations from the mean value, which are in the random range and can be accepted on the basis of the specifications, are defined. Two boundary regions are then to be defined: the upper and lower warning limits as well as the upper and lower limit values.

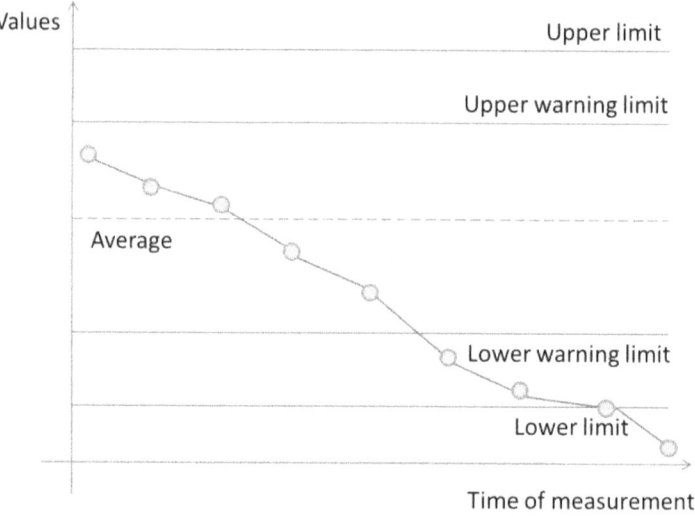

Figure 12.3 Quality control card

By recording the observed and measured values conclusions can be drawn about the course of the process:

- If the measuring points are very close to the mean value, the limit values are obviously too generous.
- If the measured values are more than seven above or below the mean value, there is no random scattering, but a systematic influence whose cause has to be analysed.
- If a trend is visible (as in Figure 12.3), the process threatens to become out of control and an intervention is to be initiated at the latest when the warning limit is exceeded. This in order to prevent waste production.

The quality control card thus proves to be a very useful tool for production process monitoring. Moreover, it prevents the occurrence of such elaborate deviations which would otherwise cause waste production.

Pareto diagram

Management always requires concentration on the essentials. Resources (financial resources, time) are scarce, which is why it is necessary to focus on those activities/projects/tasks which have the greatest impact on the company's objectives.

Lean Management makes use of tools that quickly and without great effort can be used to filter out the key points for improvement.

The Pareto analysis maps the characteristics of an object or a process by importance and thus enables the concentration on measures or projects with the greatest possible effectiveness with respect to defined targets (Fig. 12.4).

The most well-known is the so-called ABC analysis, which, for example, classifies the present articles in a warehouse according to their value in predefined classes. Typically, 20% of the items make up 80% of the total value of a warehouse.

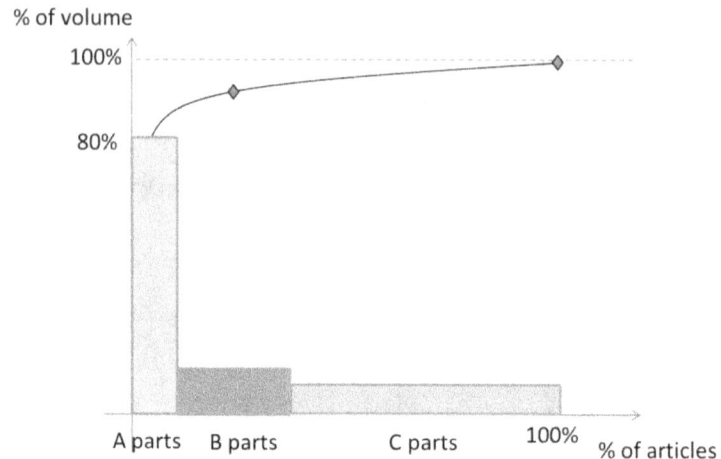

Figure 12.4 Pareto diagram

However, Pareto analysis can easily be applied to other objects or processes, such as a classification of the nature of errors in manufacturing and service processes in terms of error costs and secondary error costs.

Correlation diagram

In a correlation diagram, two changing variables are related. With this tool, one would like to find out which (linear) correlation between two statistically acquired variables exists. For example, the assumption can be checked whether the temperature of a production process has an influence on the number of defective parts.

However, what the correlation analysis cannot tell us is the meaningfulness of the relationship between the two variables. It is possible that a correlation of two variables is determined (for example dependence of the rejection rate on the lunar phase), but a causal connection has not yet been established. False conclusions are possible, which is why great caution should be paid when evaluating the diagram.

As shown in Figure 12.5, the measured values are recorded according to the collected data and visualized in a diagram. Using statistical methods, the straight line can be determined and then the so-called correlation coefficient of both variables can be calculated.

The benefit of the correlation diagram lies in the potential of the tool to reveal relationships, to qualify the direction and intensity of the context and, thus, to provide a basis for measures to improve operational conditions.

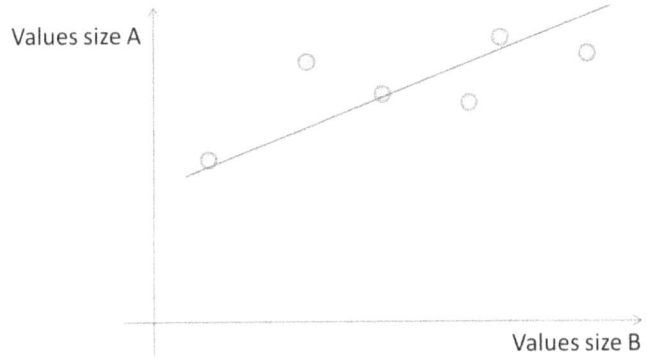

Figure 12.5 Correlation diagram

Use of a correlation diagram in production

In an engineering company, a new machine was used for the computer-controlled production of milling parts. The machine worked quite well at first, until the quotation did not increase the tolerance of corresponding parts for no apparent reason. Since the machine ran largely without the help of employees (fully automatic machine), it was placed in a room next to the production hall.

One employee initially assumed that the increasing defect rate could have to do with the onset of winter. The production manager smiled at the presumption, but had a correlation diagram prepared in which the temperature of the machine's stand and the defect rate were recorded.

The result was a clearly recognizable link. Due to the coefficient of expansion of the material used in the machine, the precision was dependent on the prevailing ambient temperature. The problem could be solved by heating the room in which the machine was installed.

Brainstorming/History chart

In a company's usual discussion and decision-making processes, the established thinking patterns and given framework of action often limit the chances of getting a completely new and innovative solution or decision. Brainstorming is a (often interdisciplinary) team which develops the desired solution in two phases.

At the beginning of the brainstorming a precise definition of the question is formulated. This is a necessary condition for successful brainstorming. The team members may need additional information about the issue under discussion. However, this information must not contain any solutions which may lead to a bias or hinder the development of entirely new ideas.

In the first phase, proposals, but also thoughts about the problem are gathered without any restrictions or criticism. This aspect is particularly important since any criticism expressed during this phase hinders the further creativity of the team members. In this phase, the focus is exclusively on the collection of a large number of ideas.

In the second phase, the suggested thoughts and ideas are first ranked and then evaluated. As a result, the thoughts and ideas that can be realized are put into action.

In practice, committing a professional presenter has proven itself. On the one hand, this precludes an advance through the company's knowledge and experience; on the other hand, a goal-oriented and project-oriented handling of the brainstorming is ensured.

Cause-effect diagram

The cause-and-effect diagram (*Ishikawa* diagram) is used for systematically examining problems and their causes (Figure 12.6). The starting point is a problem (in this example a non-timely transfer of a shipment to expedition), of which the causes are to be investigated. Both systematically and visually.

The system is achieved by defining causal categories. In practice, various main causes are provided as standard in the diagrams. Common:

- human
- machine
- material
- method

In many specialised books the following causes are added:

- measurement
- environment

Selecting the cited categories depends on the problem to be solved. Subsequently the secondary causes identified in the main category are listed.

Visualization of the main and secondary causes of operational problems supports the recognition of the main problem causes. Thus, the elaboration of problem solutions is made much easier.

The following steps are taken when the cause-effect diagram is created:

- Development of the main and secondary cause
- Verification of completeness of the causes (here the visualization is a help in the form of a diagram, since the main categories provide the essential points)
- Filtering the most important causes out (assessment of the causes according to importance, extent of influence and probability of occurrence)
- Plausibility check of the result from step four (use of statistical procedures)
- Elaboration of measures to eliminate the problem
- Implementation of the measures

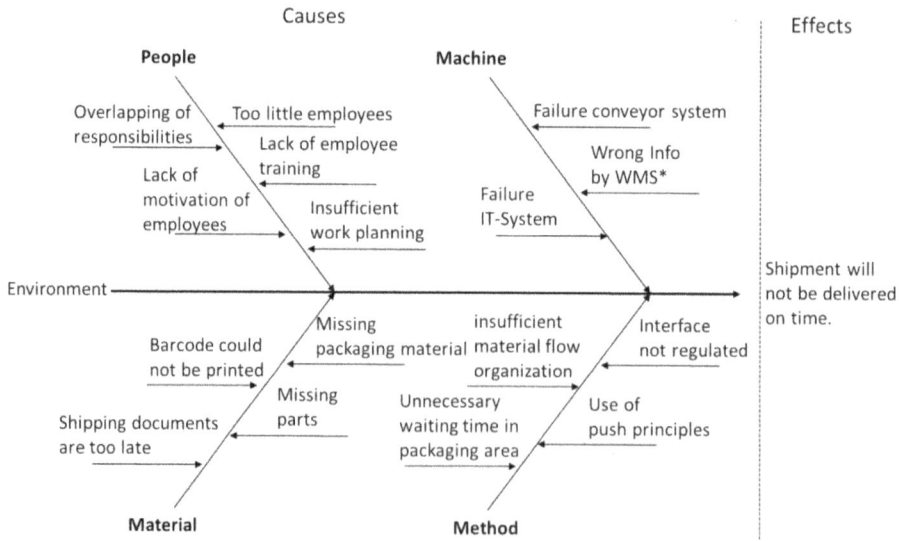

Figure 12.6 Cause-effect diagram (* WMS = Warehouse Management System)

Visualization of the problem causes the manager's attention and the employees' awareness for the problem. In addition, it is clear to what extent operational processes in daily practice are really controlled according to the company's objectives. The results of weighing the causes give clear indications at which point of the process sequence improvement measures the greatest effect could have.

12.2   M7 – Seven management tools

The seven management tools are also referred to as "New Seven Tools for Quality Management" in the specialised literature. A detailed description of the tools can be found in Kamiske and Brauer (2008b).

The management tools can be grouped according to the execution phases of projects. In the analysis and specification of problems phase, the affinity diagram (structuring verbal/qualitative statements in clear groups) and the relation diagram (structured representation of the main causes of a problem and their interactions) are used.

In the development phase, the tree diagram (elaboration of means and measures to solve the problem), the matrix diagram (analysis of the relationships and interactions of causes and measures) as well as the matrix data analysis (visual representation of three quantitative information in one portfolio diagram) are used.

In the preparatory phase of measure implementation (provision of funds, preparation of the processes), the problem-resolution plan (preparation of measures in case of unforeseen difficulties in the implementation) and the network (representation of the temporal linkage of the measures) are used.

All tools shown have following in common:

- an easily comprehensible visualization of the facts under discussion takes place,
- the complexity inherent to all problems is reduced to a manageable level,
- and the necessary knowledge about the application of tools can be acquired relatively quickly.

In this context lean means a pragmatic way to solve problems without overloading the process with elaborate methods and the necessity of trained specialists and instead only using simple tools. In this case, the road is not the goal, but the solution of upcoming problems in the company.

12.3 5-W question technique

The very thorough questioning of problems and their causes is a core component of management in Japanese companies. What seems strange at first glance is an effective method to get to the root causes of problems.

In companies, a problem is often recognized (for example, a machine loses oil), but it's symptom is being cured (the workshop master has the oil spot removed). The cause of the problem will continue (the machine will lose oil again).

Japanese managers question the deeper cause straightforwardly.

In our example, the real cause of the oil loss can be found if one consistently questions the causes six times. In most cases, you are moving upstream in the process chain. The reason for the oil leak is the purchase of inferior material which, in turn, is due to the fact that the company has exclusively used direct, quantitative and one-dimensional key figures for the flexible remuneration of its executives.

This plastic example (cf. Liker 2004, p.253) shows how the true cause can only be determined if a thorough inquiry is made. Only in this way can the problem be solved. In our example, the remuneration model for the company's executives would have to be redesigned so that not only the decision in a department (purchasing decision in purchasing department) but also impacts in other departments (in our example: additional costs in production) are taken into account. In the 5-W tracing technique, the avoidance of waste (Muda), unevenness (Mura) and overburden (Muri) is at the centre. Beyond the example given, the five W questions are asked, who, where, when, why, and how. This is an in-depth question and the causes of the problems under discussion are identified (detailed description in Brunner 2008, p.22 f.).

13. Personal commitment – conclusion

The success of a company is decisively measured by its ability to implement its strategic objectives. Lean Management is the aggressive implementation of economic requirements, which requires a methodological approach, both of employees and of management, without restrictions.

> There is no such thing as perfection, but you can strive for it!

Lean Management employs every kind of energy to test people-oriented theories for their operational viability and to question each day anew to create room for the next improvement. It puts the management and supporting departments back into their actual task of being part of the team. Lean Management shows that every position on the team can improve in various ways of waste-reduction, contributing greatly to the overall success of the company. In other words, whoever believes that the company is already producing waste-free production is wrong.

> There is no waste-free production! At the most, wastes are only reduced step by step!

Political measures are reduced or excluded, they are replaced by tasks and the welfare of the entire company and its workforce. The extreme and clear accountability of Lean Management is targeted and showing problems of the responsible areas. It is process-oriented, function-oriented. This means employees are challenged to think across their own department boundaries.

> Lean Management refers to all and does not make a hierarchical distinction!

Personal commitment – conclusion

Lean Management facilitates and empowers everyone to make their contribution to the company's value! Through its philosophy, organization and tools, it ensures that ideas and problems become obvious and recognizable and that we do not fail or give up on the difficult road to success.

Exaggerated and yet justified, Lean Management forces many managers and specialists to move back from the foreclosed offices and great strategic thinking, to put our ego aside and think in terms of the team, to listen to it and to make decisions regardless of personal preferences and pointing the way in the hard day-to-day business. From employees it demands that they actively participate in the change process and do not hinder it. Lean Management supports us in the fog of everyday business and the human challenges of maintaining and enforcing objective thinking for the benefit of the customer and the entire company, without forgetting that it's people who are at the core of success and make everything possible.

Literature

Ballé, F. and *Ballé, M.* (2007): *The Gold Mine.* Lean Enterprise Institute

Ballé, M. and *Ballé, F.* (2009): *The Lean Manager.* Lean Enterprise Institute

Brunner, F.J. (2014): *Japanische Erfolgskonzepte.* Carl Hanser Verlag

Dennis, P. (2006): *Getting the Right Things Done.* Lean Enterprise Institute

Drew, J., McCallum, B. and *Roggenhofer, S.* (2005): *Unternehmen Lean.* Campus Verlag

Füermann, T. and *Dammasch, C.* (2008): *Prozessmanagement.* Carl Hanser Verlag

Geiger, G., Hering, E. and *Kummer, R.* (2011): *Kanban.* Carl Hanser Verlag

Gorecki, P. and *Pautsch, P.* (2014): *Praxisbuch Lean Management. Der Weg zur operativen Excellence.* Carl Hanser Verlag

Hummel, T. and *Malorny, C.* (2011): *Total Quality Management.* Carl Hanser Verlag

Kamiske, G.F. and *Brauer, J.-P.* (2012): *ABC des Qualitätsmanagements.* Carl Hanser Verlag

Kamiske, G.F. and *Brauer, J.-P.* (2008): *Qualitätsmanagement von A bis Z.* Carl Hanser Verlag

Kostka, C. and *Kostka, S.* (2011): *Der Kontinuierliche Verpesserungsprozess*. Carl Hanser Verlag

Liker, J.K. (2004): *The Toyota Way*. McGraw-Hill

Matyas, K. (2013): *Taschenbuch der Instandhaltungslogistik*. Carl Hanser Verlag

Ohno, T. (1993): *Das Toyota Produktionssystem*. Campus Verlag

Pautsch, P. (2010): "*Erschließung von Rationalisierungspotenzialen im Lager durch Lean Management*". In: *Productivity Management 3/2010*, p. 43 – 46

Rother, M. (2010): *Toyota Kata*. McGraw-Hill

Shingo, S. (1986): *Zero Quality Control*. Productivity Press

Womack, J.P. und *Jones, D.T.* (2003): *Lean Thinking*. Free Press

www.ingramcontent.com/pod-product-compliance
Lightning Source LLC
Chambersburg PA
CBHW071421210526
45465CB00001B/482